Fat Tire
Wisconsin

A Mountain Bike Trail Guide

D1023374

A Mountain Bike Trail Guide

Second edition

W. Chad McGrath
and
Mark Parman

The University of Wisconsin Press

The University of Wisconsin Press
2537 Daniels Street
Madison, Wisconsin 53718

3 Henrietta Street
London WC2E 8LU, England

1   3   5   4   2

Printed in the United States of America

Library of Congress Cataloging-in-Publication Data
McGrath, Wm. Chad.
Fat tire Wisconsin : a mountain bike trail guide /
W. Chad McGrath and Mark Parman. —2nd ed.
            pp.   cm.
Includes index.
ISBN 0-299-17214-7 (pbk. : alk. paper)
1. All terrain cycling—Wisconsin—Guidebooks.
2. Bicycle trails—Wisconsin—Guidebooks.
3. Wisconsin—Guidebooks.
I. Parman, Mark. II. Title.
GV1045.5.W6 M34   2001
796.6'3'09775—dc21   00-011981

Contents

The Central Trails

Central Shorts

The Southern Trails

Southern Shorts

Fat Tire Wisconsin Trails Sites

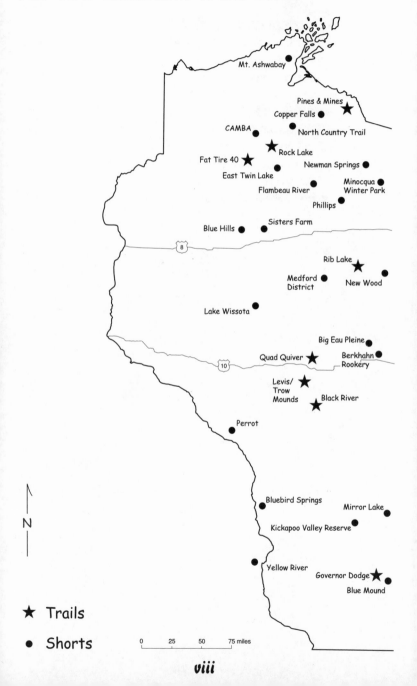

Mt. Ashwabay ●

Pines & Mines ★
Copper Falls ●
CAMBA ● North Country Trail ●
Rock Lake ★
Fat Tire 40 ★ Newman Springs ●
East Twin Lake ●
Flambeau River ● Minocqua Winter Park ●
Phillips ●

Blue Hills ● Sisters Farm ●

8

Rib Lake ★
Medford District ● New Wood ●

Lake Wissota ●

Big Eau Pleine ●
Quad Quiver ★ Berkhahn Rookery ●
10
Levis/Trow Mounds ★
Black River ★

Perrot ●

Bluebird Springs ●
Mirror Lake ●
Kickapoo Valley Reserve ●

Yellow River ●
Governor Dodge ★
Blue Mound ●

N

★ Trails

● Shorts

0   25   50   75 miles

viii

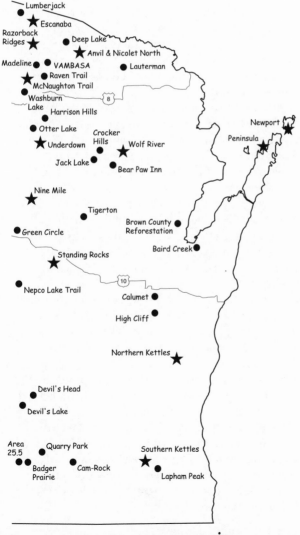

Lumberjack
Escanaba
Razorback Ridges
Deep Lake
Anvil & Nicolet North
Madeline
VAMBASA
Lauterman
Raven Trail
McNaughton Trail
Washburn Lake
Harrison Hills
Otter Lake
Crocker Hills
Newport
Underdown
Wolf River
Peninsula
Jack Lake
Bear Paw Inn
Nine Mile
Tigerton
Brown County Reforestation
Green Circle
Baird Creek
Standing Rocks
Nepco Lake Trail
Calumet
High Cliff
Northern Kettles
Devil's Head
Devil's Lake
Area 25.5
Quarry Park
Southern Kettles
Badger Prairie
Cam-Rock
Lapham Peak

8

10

Preface

In the early 1980s, I started off-roading on a cyclocross bike, mainly on hiking trails at a nearby city park. By today's standards, my bike was crude—a Raleigh road frame fitted with knobby tires, cantilever brakes, low gearing, and bar-end shifters. It rode like a fully loaded hay wagon, especially when the ground was frozen. The skinny, high-pressure knobbies and the rigid fork didn't do much to smooth the ride.

That didn't matter much, though, because I enjoyed just riding in the woods, particularly in autumn. Back then mountain bikes weren't the popular machines they are now; they were mostly cult bikes or faddish machines. A few people in town owned cobbled together mountain bikes, and Gary Fisher and friends had long been tearing down the side of Mount Tamalpais on their renowned cruisers. Mountain biking stood on the brink of its imminent explosion. At that time, however, people couldn't walk into a shop, plunk down the cash and buy a mountain bike. Of course, the Midwest has always been a bit behind both coasts. So we improvised and rode modified road machines.

Even though we lacked suspension, twenty-seven speeds, index-shifting, carbon fiber, and titanium—all the high-end things many take for granted today—we still had a ball. In a way, I enjoyed off-road riding more back then. We had the trails to ourselves, sharing them with an occasional hiker or jogger. We were pioneers of sorts.

Today, mountain biking is bona fide recreation, an official sport, now an Olympic sport. Television ads—Mountain Dew comes to mind—often feature a mountain bike or two. Fat tires have permeated American culture in a way the road bike never did and probably never will.

Along with the official recognition have come problems. All those new riders on the trails led inevitably to conflicts with other users, most notably the hiking and equestrian groups. Trail postings and closings followed. A friend tells me of riding, in the mid-1980s, the entire length of the Ice Age Trail in the Southern Kettle Moraine State Forest, a two-day ride. Just ten years later, mountain bikers can only ride a fraction of the trails in the Southern Kettles and no section of the Ice Age Trail. The times have changed.

A decade ago we rode from our houses, pedaling to the trails and back. I still ride to some of my favorite haunts—those secret spots close to town—but for the most part, the sport of mountain biking has become a destination sport. Many mountain bikers and many readers of this trail guide live in urban areas, far from the woods and far from the trails. So the bike rack has become a necessary evil. However, I encourage readers to find those secret close-to-home spots, those places we can ride to from the back door, that single-track on the way home from work, so our sport isn't merely one of destination.

We've ridden lots of trails around the state, those in this book, plus others, and have written a second edition of *Fat Tire Wisconsin* to help folks make informed decisions about those destinations. Since our first edition several new trails have either opened or been developed, and we are pleased to see this progression. The southern part of the state can boast of several new systems—good news down there. Inside, we recommend some of the state's best places for riding. I hope you'll have a chance to ride several, if not all, of these off-road destinations. And I hope you continue frequenting those trails close to home.

—Mark

My introduction to mountain biking came as a gift, in the form of a brand-new Maruishi bike. My partner, M. J., decided that since I loved cross-country skiing, I would also love riding the same trails on a bike. She was correct. In the fall of 1985, after getting the bike for my March birthday, I rode my first Chequamegon Fat Tire 40. I finished in five hours, ten minutes, and twenty-seven seconds, slightly less than three hours off the winning pace. M. J. never said I'd be fast.

When Mark asked me to help write this book, I figured it would offer a good excuse to get back to riding more. It has. My bones bounce just like old times. Here's hoping what we've written gets you jiggling more too.

—Chad

Introduction

Besides riding responsibly, joining WORBA (the Wisconsin Off-Road Bicycle Association) is one of the best ways to promote mountain biking in this state. WORBA promotes our sport by opening new trails, organizing trail workdays, monitoring issues that affect mountain biking, and speaking up for us politically. At a grassroots level, WORBA has several local chapters throughout the state that focus their efforts on local trails; at the global level, WORBA is allied with IMBA (the International Mountain Bike Association) to promote the good of our sport.

Both groups advocate responsible mountain bike riding, for both nonmembers and members. If we ride like idiots and provoke hikers, hunters, cross-country skiers, and equestrians—the people we have things in common with—then we will lose trails. It's that simple. For this reason WORBA endorses IMBA's rules of the trail:

1. Ride on open trails only.
2. Leave no trace.
3. Control your bicycle.
4. Always yield trail.
5. Never spook animals.
6. Plan ahead.

For more information about WORBA, contact them at P.O. Box 1681, Madison, Wisconsin 53701-1681 or at www.worba.org.

Selection Criteria

One of the most difficult tasks in writing a trail guide is deciding which trails to include and which to leave out. Some of our inclusions were obvious choices, others not so obvious. In the end, we included sixty-eight trails.

No mountain bike trail guide of the Badger State would be complete without certain trails. The Chequamegon Area Mountain Bike Association (CAMBA) trails, the 300-plus miles of trail winding through national forest, had to be in the book. As did the Southern Kettle Moraine Forest's Emma Carlin and John Muir loops, which see more mountain bikes each season than any other trail in the state. Levis/Trow Mounds, Razorback Ridges, and Nine Mile County Forest, all with miles of extraordinary singletrack, had to go in as well.

Then there are the less obvious choices, places that aren't well known, places like the Ice Age Trail in the Harrison Hills, new singletrack at the Bear Paw Inn, Area 25.5, the Medford District of the Chequamegon National Forest, and Big Eau Pleine County Park. We rode these somewhat obscure locations, and they pleasantly surprised us.

What specific criteria did we use? We weighed trail location, length, type, condition, marking, and mapping. But don't get the idea that we were entirely objective, using point systems and calculators to pick trails. The final measure leading to inclusion in the book was whether we liked the trail, in the end a rather subjective approach.

We hope you find your favorite trail in *Fat Tire Wisconsin*. If not, let us know, and we'll come ride it and consider it for a future edition. Write to us c/o the University of Wisconsin Press.

Book Layout

We divided the book into three sections, representing three geographical regions. The North section covers trails north of Highway 8. The Central section includes trails south of Highway 8, but north of Highway 10. The South section details trails south of Highway 10.

We further divided our treatment of trail systems into long and short. We treated the longs, the premier mountain bike destinations in the state, with two pages of text and a two-page map. The shorts received briefer treatment, but not necessarily because they are worse places to ride. We felt some of the trails in the shorts lacked sufficient mileage or enough varied terrain or weren't sufficiently scenic. At others, trail conditions were subpar or the trail was poorly marked or not marked at all. Many obscure and unofficial places were included in the shorts category, and some readers will no doubt prefer riding these seldom ridden trails. Some are hidden gems.

Safety and Being Nice to Others

This book doesn't include a section on how to ride, what to wear, what to bring along, or how to make trailside repairs. Those things readers should learn or know before setting out. We're assuming that readers know how to fix a flat or ride with those who do know and that you'll bring along a spare tube and a pump.

If a trail system warranted extraordinary gear, we suggested that in the text. For instance, if a trail wound through big country, we suggested a familiarization with USGS (United States Geological Survey) maps and a compass. To get USGS topographical maps write the Geological and Natural History Survey, University of Wisconsin–Extension, 3817 Mineral Point Road, Madison, Wisconsin 53705-5100. If you don't own a *Wisconsin Atlas and Gazetteer*, published by DeLorme, consider buying one. It's simply the best atlas of the state—you'll discover places you didn't know existed.

While we love to ride, doing so during gun deer season can be foolish, even if you dress in blaze orange. If you must ride, be sure it's in an area that's at least closed to hunting with rifles. Some trails receive a lot of hunting pressure during small game season, which usually begins the same day as the Chequamegon Fat Tire Festival, the third Saturday in September. The Yellow Loop at the Northern Kettle Moraine State Forest, for instance, is closed during small game season.

Be courteous to other trail users, like hikers, runners, equestrians, and hunters. We share many of the same desires and similar agendas. We all face shrinking landscapes and losses of trail and habitat. We should work together to combat development and the encroachment of urban blight, the things that threaten us all.

Terms

Singletrack: We used this word to describe what we felt was true singletrack—the stuff that winds around granite boulders and between trees with barely enough room for the handlebar. Two bikes cannot fit side-by-side on singletrack, which looks and feels very much like a deer trail.

Doubletrack: Also known as two-track, this is trail generally too wide to be called singletrack, including logging roads, fire roads, and many ski trails. We refer to some roads as doubletrack but always describe the road's surface, whether it's pavement or rock or dirt.

ATB: All Terrain Bicycle. We felt it was a more accurate acronym than the more popular MTB for Mountain Bike.

Other Stuff

We employed the measure, miles or kilometers, that each particular trail system used. Most of the trails that double as cross-country ski trails use kilometers.

Whither the "We"? The "we" refers to a variety of people, not just the authors. Other riders joined us for many of our rides, and we thank them for their company. Mark's Weimaraner, Gunnar, dog-tested many of the trails. Too bad he can't talk and tell us his favorite. We know for sure he likes the singletrack at Nine Mile.

Important Websites

A couple commercial sites that catalog trails in Wisconsin are www.trailmonkey.com and www.gearhead.com. You can find information about the state's mountain bike advocacy group at www.worba.org. A list of Wisconsin state parks, forests, and trails can be found at www.danenet.wicip.org /bcp/wspft.

Mt. Ashwabay

Copper Falls

North Country Trail

CAMBA

Lumberjack

East Twin Lake

Newman
Springs

Minocqua
Winter
Park

Deep Lake

Flambeau River

VAMBASA

Phillips

Madeline

Raven Trail

Lauterman

Washburn
Lake

Blue Hills

Sisters Farm

8

8

10

45

The
Northern
Trails

Anvil and Nicolet North

The Civilian Conservation Corps (CCC), known also as Roosevelt's Forest Army, laid out the Anvil Trail in the 1930s, so it's one of the oldest recreational trails in the state. Originally a hiking trail, then a cross-country ski trail, the Anvil also makes for excellent mountain biking. With twenty kilometers of doubletrack at Anvil and another twenty-five kilometers at Nicolet North to the south (the Eagle River Nordic X-C trails in winter) ATBers can definitely make a day of it riding one or both trails.

Few trails give the feeling of traveling through the Big Woods like the Anvil does. Four short runs originate at the trailhead off Highway 70: the East and West Trails, Nine Mile Run, and the infamous Devil's Run. This beautiful 2.5-kilometer trail sports horns and a pitchfork, in the guise of steep climbs and gnarly exposed roots. We pushed our bikes up two climbs on Devil's Run, even though we repeatedly tried to make them without dismounting. Roots and a few rocks jar bike and rider the entire length of the trail. Front suspension isn't absolutely necessary here, but it's sure a lot more comfortable than going rigid.

Devil's Run isn't all pain and suffering, though. The thrill of the downhills almost makes up for the pain of the uphills, and the hemlocks bordering the trail tower overhead and provide a holy, cathedral-like experience—devil be damned.

A small cabin, stocked with plenty of dry firewood and a couple of picnic tables, waits at the southern end of Devil's Run at the junction of several trails. It's a good place to rest, snack, or spend the night.

The 3-kilometer Lake Loop starts at the cabin junction and skirts Upper Nine Mile Lake. There are fewer majestic trees and more deer flies on this short section, but it's still worth riding. The two-way trail to the left eventually crosses bubbly Nine Mile Creek, where we accidentally spooked a mating pair of Cooper's Hawks, and comes out on Forest Road 2460. Another trailhead and parking lot lies directly right, or to the south. This trailhead sits between Anvil and Nicolet North—the place to park if planning to ride both trail systems. Forest Road 2460 intersects Highway 70 two miles east of the Anvil trailhead.

The 5-kilometer Pat Shay Trail is the most difficult as well as most scenic trail at Nicolet North, winding through several dense stands of huge hemlock and along the banks of namesake Pat Shay Lake. The trail along the banks rises and falls almost as precipitously as does Devil's Run; it's no ride along a flat beach.

The trails at Nicolet North aren't marked as well as those at Anvil, nor are they ridden as much. We saw no tire tracks other than our own. This solitude can be both good and bad. Good, for obvious reasons. Bad, because in some open areas the grasses grew knee-high due to lack of traffic. The grass jammed our derailleurs and clogged our chainrings and freewheels.

We did find true singletrack off the Pat Shay Trail, which we ultimately realized was the Hidden Lakes Trail, a 13-mile hiking trail with untapped potential for mountain biking. Local riders claim there's plenty of singletrack, nearly 30 miles in the area, but you'll have to find it. Sorry, we promised we wouldn't publish where it is. Contact the NOBS (the Nicolet Off-Road Bicycle Society) or Perry Sippl at Chain of Lakes Cyclery on Highway 45 in Eagle River. Thanks to Jeff Herrett, at the Eagle River Ranger Station, for his help.

Directions: Anvil Trail is 8.5 miles east of Eagle River on the south side of Highway 70. For information contact Eagle River Ranger District, Nicolet National Forest, P.O. Box 1809, 4364 Wall Street, Eagle River, Wisconsin 54521. Telephone is 715-479-2827.

Fee: There's a parking fee of $3 per day or $10 per season.

Anvil Trail

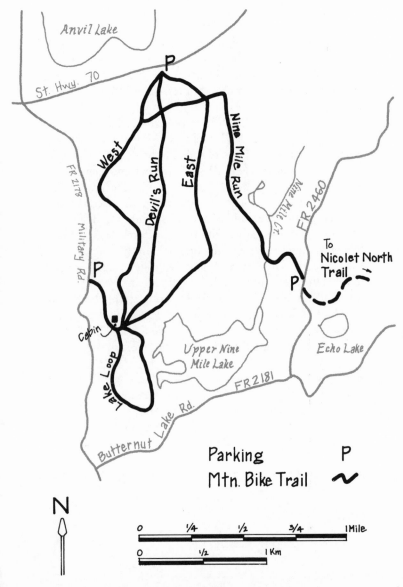

Anvil Lake

St. Hwy. 70

FR 2178

Military Rd.

West

Devil's Run

East

Nine Mile Run

P

Nine Mile Cr.

FR 2460

To Nicolet North Trail

P

P

Cabin

Lake Loop

Upper Nine Mile Lake

Echo Lake

FR 2181

Butternut Lake Rd.

Parking   P

Mtn. Bike Trail   ∿

N

0   1/4   1/2   3/4   1 Mile

0   1/2   1 Km

Nicolet North Trail

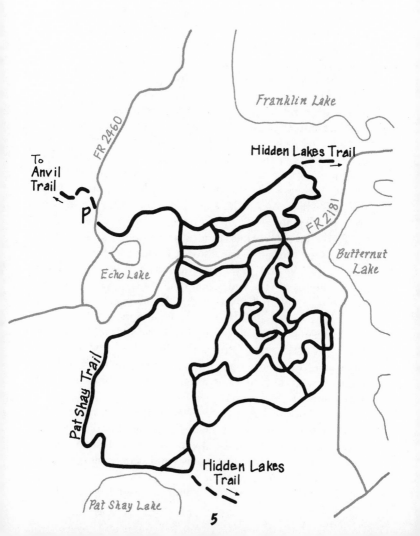

Franklin Lake

FR 2460

Hidden Lakes Trail

To
Anvil
Trail

P

FR 2181

Butternut
Lake

Echo Lake

Pat Shay Trail

Hidden Lakes
Trail

Pat Shay Lake

Fat Tire 40

Each September 2,500 riders take part in the Chequamegon Fat Tire Festival, the largest off-road event in the country. Part of the Festival's popularity stems from the challenging but accessible course. Although the course changes slightly from year to year, depending on rainfall, we've included the 2000 edition with a few variations.

The race starts each year near the National Guard Armory in downtown Hayward and winds out of town east on Highway 77. The race really begins when the course enters the grass trail through Rosie's Field, where the lead riders launch the first serious attacks of the race. This is where LeMond blew the 1992 race apart. For those wanting to skip the pavement out of Hayward, begin at the CAMBA (Chequamegon Area Mountain Bike Association) trailhead on Mosquito Brook Road, which is about six miles into the course.

Here the Birkebeiner Trail, a thirty-foot-wide ski trail, intersects the Mosquito Brook Road. The ski trail runs roughly northeast a mile and a half, then turns right onto Phipps Fire Lane. Phipps, a wide and sandy doubletrack, runs six miles north to County Highway OO. A right on County OO takes riders back to the Birkie Trail. Another option is the long, rolling section of Birkie Trail, which runs from Mosquito Brook to OO, and ultimately Telemark Lodge. The Birkebeiner Foundation maintains a chalet (another CAMBA trailhead) with running water at the intersection of the ski trail and County OO.

A worthwhile detour for the especially hungry and thirsty would be left on OO down the hill three miles to the town of Seeley, home of the Sawmill Saloon. The Sawmill Saloon gathers loggers and builders with cyclists and skiers—buffalo plaid and lycra mix surprisingly well.

Take OO back east from Phipps or west from the OO

chalet to Janet Road (west of the Birkie Trail) and follow Janet as it winds north to more hilly sections of the race course and intersects Boedecker Road at CAMBA marker S5. Take Boedecker right, or east, and cross the Birkie Trail. Past the ski trail at a T intersection turn right on Spider Lake Road (also called Telemark Road) onto the Lake Helane Loop of the CAMBA system. This loop meanders by Smith Lake then Lake Helaine, two gems that most Fat Tire Festival riders miss because they've got their heads down, grinding away, following the knobby tire ahead.

This route follows Snowmobile Trail 77 down a steep, rocky descent. One mile beyond Smith Lake, go right at the T intersection, and this eventually winds past Lake Helaine, still following the CAMBA loop. Past the lake, turn left, and two more lefts bring you to Spider Lake Road, marked intersection S20 on CAMBA maps. Follow the trail left here.

This loop intersects the Seeley Fire Tower Road (S17) and the infamous stair-step climb up to the old fire tower site. From here, there's a long view of the Namekagon River Valley to the west. Turn left and descend the road coming up Fire Tower Hill, against the grain of the CAMBA markers. The Birkebeiner Trail also parallels this road. At the bottom (S12), turn right onto CAMBA's Fire Tower Loop. Go right at the next intersection (C20) on the Fire Tower Trail, which then intersects the Birkie Trail (C21), becoming the Short and Fat Loop. The Short and Fat eventually merges with Telemark Road (a.k.a. Spider Lake Road), one of the fastest parts of the race, the place where things really heat up.

Follow the CAMBA markers, going right at C7. This trail, Spring Creek Trail, intersects the road to Telemark Lodge (C10), and a left will head back to the lodge. Numerous ski trails (designed for a World Cup race in the 1970s) wind around and among the sharp hills south and west of the lodge. Check these out if your legs still have some spring in them.

Directions: The Mosquito Brook trailhead is four miles north of Hayward on Highway 63. Turn right at the CAMBA marker and follow Mosquito Brook Road approximately two miles to the trailhead. Telemark Lodge is located three miles east of Cable on County Highway M. For detailed maps contact CAMBA at P.O. Box 141, Cable, Wisconsin 54821. Telephone is 800-533-7454 and website is www.cable4fun.com/camba.

Fat Tire 40 Trail

SEELEY

Co. Hwy. OO

Match Line

Phipps Fire Lane

PHIPPS

32

31

30

33

34

Mosquito Bk. Rd.

U.S. 63

HAYWARD

35

36

37

St. Hwy. 77

39

38

Rosie's Field

N

0   1   2   3 Miles

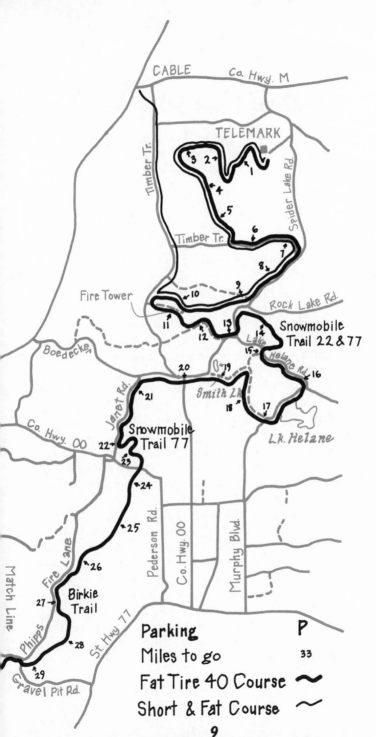

CABLE   Co. Hwy. M

TELEMARK

Timber Tr.

3   2   1

4

5

6

Timber Tr.

7

8

Spider Lake Rd.

9

10

Fire Tower

Rock Lake Rd.

11

12   13   14

Lake   Snowmobile
Trail 22 & 77

15

Helane Rd.

16

Boedecker

20   19

Janet Rd.

21   Smith Lk.

18   17

Co. Hwy. OO

22   Snowmobile
Trail 77

L.k. Helane

23

24

Pederson Rd.

25

Co. Hwy. OO

Murphy Blvd.

Fire Lane

26

27   Birkie
Trail

Phipps

28

St. Hwy 77

Match Line

29

Gravel Pit Rd.

Parking   **P**

Miles to go   33

Fat Tire 40 Course ∼

Short & Fat Course ∼

9

Escanaba Lake

Escanaba Lake Trail, part of the VAMBASA (Vilas Area Mountain Bike and Ski Association) system, has been around for a long time and is an old favorite of hikers and cross-country skiers. For ATBers it offers ten miles of mostly singletrack through some of the prettiest northwoods scenery in Wisconsin. Some enthusiasts also bring their fishing gear. The Escanaba Lakes area has been a special DNR study area for over a decade. Its lakes have special fishing seasons and bag limits that have produced some unique fish-size populations. All fishermen must stop in at the ranger station near the parking area to register and get a permit before fishing.

The trail is a big irregular shaped ellipse intersected by two lines across its width, which create three loops. A ride around the perimeter is both scenic and challenging. Start at the parking lot off Nebish Road. Bear left out of the lot. The first mile or so is the most demanding, with quick ups and downs, and lots of tree roots. The narrow trail will challenge. The hill down to Pallette Lake is long and requires a sharp turn at the bottom.

Ridge riding for the next mile offers some views of Pallette Lake to the right. Rounding the imaginary corner and heading back east, look for and admire the several large white pine. A couple, touchable from the trail, are over nine feet in circumference. Pallette Lake is still on the right. Its shoreline is worth a visit. Hop off and check out the view.

About a half mile down the trail from the pines is a shelter. It's a three-sided, Adirondack-type, complete with fire ring The wood box reliably contains matches, paper, kindling, and firewood, all ready for burning. Bring some food and have a picnic.

The trail divides here. To the right is the parking lot, about a mile away. Go straight and continue the perimeter ride, about four more miles. Half a mile from the shelter there's a gradual downhill that leads to a wooden bridge built across a little creek that connects Lost Canoe Lake on the left with Escanaba Lake, which isn't visible at that moment. The view of Lost Canoe Lake on the left is great and lasts for a quarter mile or so until the trail turns up and away from the lake.

Escanaba Lake soon appears on the right. There are several short, steep hills before a steep downhill that ends at the junction with the Lumberjack Trail. Lumberjack traces an eleven-mile path all the way to Boulder Junction. It can be wet and overgrown with grasses, so don't choose it unless you're ready to ride long and hard.

About half a mile after Lumberjack, there's a decision to make. The trail to the left loops out and along old logging roads, perhaps some very old narrow gauge railroad grade. To the right is newer trail, which affords a couple of lake views, but also cuts through recently logged woods.

After the two sections reconnect, the trail crosses Nebish Road twice. Unpaved Nebish Road offers an easier route back if the deer flies are bad. Beware of the last couple hundred yards of trail—just before reaching the parking area, it dips down a steep, rocky grade with two ninety-degree turns. If you miss the second turn you'll still reach the parking area, only via an airborne route through some birch and maple. Good luck!

Directions: From Boulder Junction, take County Highway M south four miles, turn left, or east, on Nebish Road. The parking lot is three and a half miles ahead on the left.

Fee: Donations can be placed in ski-fee box. Technically there is no fee.

Escanaba Lake Trails

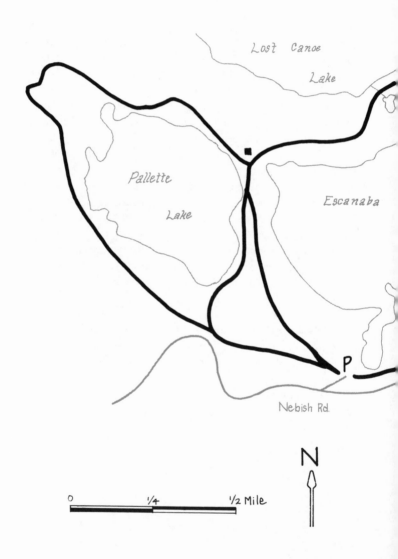

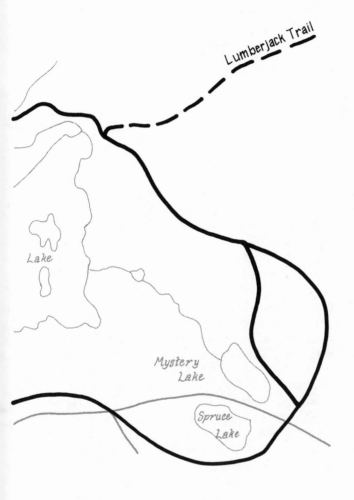

Lumberjack Trail

Lake

Mystery
Lake

Spruce
Lake

Parking   P
Mtn. Bike Trail ~
Shelter   ∎

McNaughton Trail

McNaughton Trail is narrow, suitable for riding single file, although slightly wider than most singletrack at places like Nine Mile. It's a wonderful trail that circles three lakes: Hawk, Helen, and McNaughton. Envision the trail as five imperfectly shaped circles, three on the west, two on the east, all sharing a common middle. A sixth large circle appended to the other five by a crisscross encompasses McNaughton Lake, farthest to the south.

We suggest starting out down the northernmost loop and tracing the outside of the trail. At every intersection, turn right. About a mile into the ride make the longest climb of the entire ride. The trail hooks to the right and the top is not visible from the bottom. After the next intersection, look for some of the big old stumps that dot the forest. There's one very close to the trail on the left. These are remnants from logging that took place before the area was part of the state forest. This is an area of deep, dark woods, where little light penetrates to the forest floor. Look to the side. Notice the hundreds, even thousands of small tree trunks. Then look for the big trunks that lurk here and there amid the hemlock saplings. Mostly white pine, these larger trees form the canopy that shelters all the other trees underneath. They tower one hundred feet overhead.

The five circles of trail north of McNaughton Lake are all sheltered by big conifers. These trees date from before the turn of the century and must have been saplings when the first loggers passed through. White pine over six feet around are common, as are big red pine and one hemlock that is more than three feet in diameter.

Decades of fallen needles cover the trail making a thick, spongy cushion. It's not exactly soft, like sand is soft. The riding is easy. But it is like a carpet, forgiving and quiet. Cross-country skis over snow are noisy in comparison. Imagine, as you round a sharp corner, surprising a deer, or another biker, or a black bear!

Helen Lake, located in the southwesternmost trail circle, doesn't have an access for boats. Those who want to catch its bass and panfish must get there without motors. Even if you don't fish, take at least a minute from your bike ride to enjoy a view of its lovely shoreline.

One of the system's longest downhill runs is located on the trail south of Helen Lake. It's about three hundred yards long, not steep but steady. It ends at the junction of two other trails. There's a three-sided, Adirondack-type shelter located there, complete with fire ring and firewood. Bring some food and have a picnic.

From the shelter the trail makes a 3.5-mile loop around McNaughton Lake. The ride offers varied terrain, part of it on a road that accesses the lake's public boat launch. It also traverses a couple hundred feet of boardwalk, constructed over a low area and crossing a small creek that drains from the lake. The view from this boardwalk is to the west and can be spectacular as the sun splashes into the lake.

Make a day of it, or ride the trail for a few hours. McNaughton is an outdoor wonder and one of our favorite places.

Directions: From Lake Tomahawk take Highway 47 three miles south to Kildare Road. Take Kildare west half a mile to the parking lot on the left. For information contact the DNR Office, 4125 County Highway M, Boulder Junction, Wisconsin 54512. Telephone is 715-385-2727.

Fee: Donations can be placed in ski-fee box. There is technically no fee.

McNaughton Trails

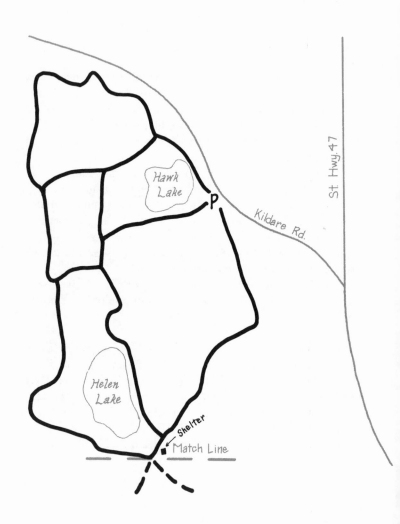

Hawk Lake

P

Kildare Rd.

St. Hwy. 47

Helen Lake

Shelter

Match Line

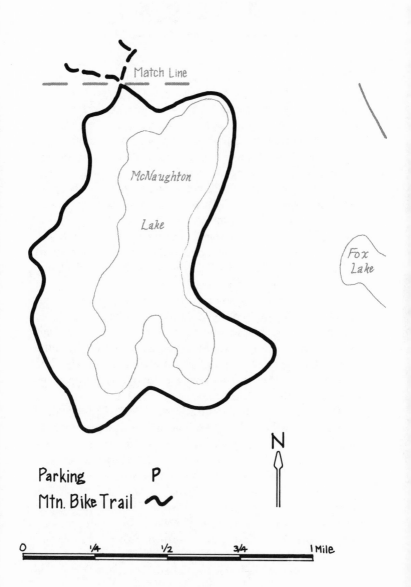

Match Line

McNaughton

Lake

Fox
Lake

Parking   P

Mtn. Bike Trail ~

N

0   1/4   1/2   3/4   1 Mile

Pines and Mines

The Pines and Mines Mountain Bike Trail System is one of the newest in the state. Actually two states since it reaches next door into the Upper Peninsula of Michigan with trails at the Porcupine Mountains and around Henry and Pomeroy Lakes. With an advertised two hundred miles of mapped and marked trails, Pines and Mines approaches CAMBA as the longest system in the state, no small undertaking for a first time venture.

Unfortunately, trail difficulty, marking, and mapping don't come close to CAMBA level. Almost all trails run on wide doubletrack or gravel roads. Some of the routes use blacktop. Only Trail 13 (Hogs Back) and parts of Trail 6 (the trails could stand more creative names) from Montreal to Weber Lake—perhaps twenty miles total—will challenge experienced riders.

What makes this system worth riding isn't the trails but the Big Snow Country the trails pass through. (This area receives up to two hundred inches of snow per year.) The hills here rise directly from Lake Superior, most impressive at the Elcho Mountain Bike Complex south of the Porkies. The country is riddled with fast-moving, clear rivers rushing head-long down to the big lake.

We experienced the Potato River firsthand, first fording it on Sullivan Road (Trail 6) then viewing the impressive Potato River Falls, south of Gurney off Highway 169. We started our ride parking at Weber Lake off County Highway E, near Whitecap Ski Hill. We took County E west to Highway 122, then took that right, or north, around the Whitecap Mountains. This road eventually winds into Saxon and past the Bear Trap Inn. Pavement the whole way, but we were enjoying the day nevertheless. North of Saxon, Trail 3 runs down to Lake Superior. Instead we took a gravel road west which intersected Highway 169, where we went left and into the town of Gurney. South of Gurney we took a gravel road marked by a Potato River Falls arrow pointing west.

Little did we know how impressive the falls would be, all ninety feet of the churning, pounding Potato crashing over rocks bigger than boxcars. There we got our first and only taste of singletrack (about one hundred meters worth) on the footpath leading down to the scenic overlook. We quickly dismounted and walked when the trail steepened beyond our skills.

Back on 169 we took Vogues Road left, or east. Two miles later this road makes a sharp ten mile per hour corner. After a dead end sign, the gravel becomes dirt doubletrack and then plunges into the icy Potato River. None of this is marked on the map. Fortunately, the river came only up to our knees, easily fordable. Three miles later this gravel intersects Highway 122 and climbs up and around Whitecap. County E brought us back to our car.

In a few spots we had trouble locating the blue route markers (identical to CAMBA's) but the map (available from the visitor centers in both Hurley and Ironwood, Michigan) was somewhat helpful, even if a bit vague.

This is a first time venture remember, and mapping and marking should improve. Hopefully. We suggest some definitive loops and more difficult trail. The land—enough to get lost in for days—is here. The people at Trek and Trail in Ironwood can help riders find local singletrack. Call 906-932-5858 for directions or locations of the weekly rides, which we hear are a whole lot of fun.

Directions: Hurley is located at the northern end of Highway 51. For information contact Pines and Mines Mountain Bike Trail System, P.O. Box 97, Hurley, Wisconsin 54534. Telephone is 800-659-3232.

Fee: None.

Pines and Mines Trails

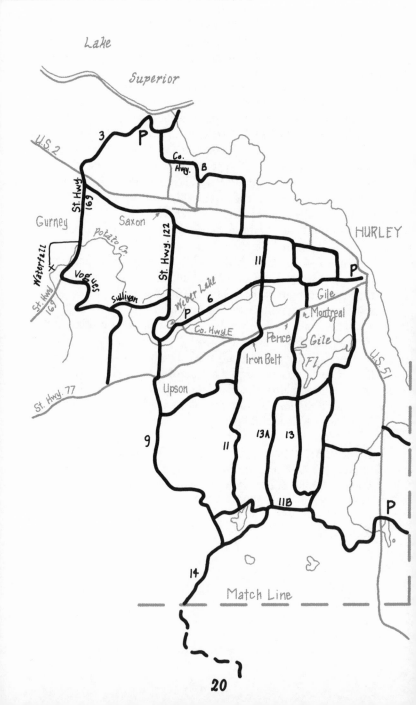

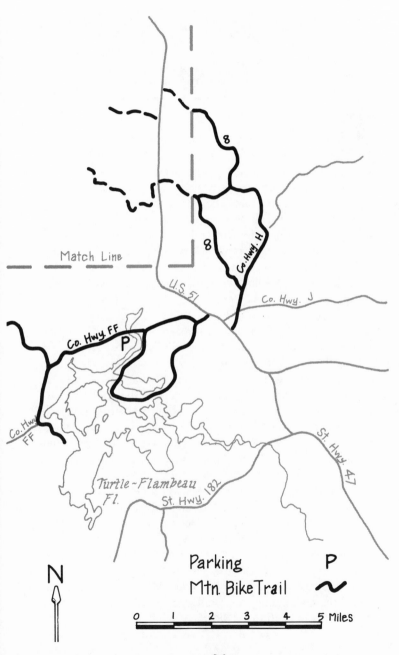

Match Line

8

8

Co. Hwy. H

U.S. 51

Co. Hwy. J

Co. Hwy. FF

P

Co. Hwy. FF

St. Hwy. 47

Turtle~Flambeau
Fl.

St. Hwy. 182

N

Parking

Mtn. Bike Trail

P

0   1   2   3   4   5 Miles

21

Razorback Ridges

Razorback Ridges, in the midst of the Northern Highland State Forest, lies fifteen miles from the Wisconsin–Upper Michigan border. The trails wind through a Northwoods land of blue lakes, sharp ridges, and intimate valleys. For most of us, Razorback is a long haul north. Of any Wisconsin off-road destination, however, it's the one worth filling the gas tank and pointing the car north for.

The Ridges consists of an agreeable mix of doubletrack and true singletrack, about thirty miles total. The well-marked trails range from flat to rolling to steep, so riders of all abilities can find pleasing terra firma.

The easiest loops—Doug's Folly, Roller Coaster, and Ridge Trail—will challenge most riders. Although these trails may not demand above average technical skill, they do demand aerobic fitness since the doubletrack rolls up and down, often steeply, crossing and following the hogback terrain.

Many cyclists ride Razorback because of the wonderful singletrack and country that these twisting trails trek through. Rat'l Snake, off Long Rider (at 12.7 kilometers, the longest trail in the system) will wear out your granny-gear. And wear out your brakes as well. Bruce's Mountain (blame your aches, pains, and mishaps on trail developer Bruce Drew) will definitely shoot up levels of both lactate and adrenaline. Most of the singletrack originates off Long Rider. Blueberry Lake Loop veers off Snooker's Nook, a short doubletrack off Long Rider. This trail winds past Blueberry Lake, twisting and turning around granite rocks and pine roots, and eventually runs into Rat'L Snake. Snomo's Trail also strikes off Snooker's Nook. This section of singletrack runs past the larger Muskellunge Lake and enters the main trail system on Turnagain Arm, another short doubletrack loop off Long Rider.

Campers can reach the DNR-run Crystal Lake Campground from this section of Snomo's Trail. The Pine Forest Trail—a relatively easy singletrack, groomed for classic skiing in winter—connects to Long Rider, a bit farther down the trail from Blueberry. Starrett Lake campers can enter Razorback from this trail. Those wanting an extended stay can camp and ride directly to the trails from these campgrounds. Weekend camping gets tight, though.

Farther east, the Duck Lake Loop veers off Long Rider. This, too, is relatively easy singletrack, a short one-kilometer jaunt through red and white pine and around tiny Duck Lake. The pine needles often covering this mostly flat trail help cushion the ride, a bonus for those on rigid bikes. Besides the crazy, twisting descent on Rat'L Snake, the only other scares come from Hair Raiser and Suicide Hill, both aptly named. The steepest descent on Hair Raiser is mostly a straight shot down smooth doubletrack, requiring only a bit of nerve to conquer. Suicide Hill isn't as tame, with its infamous hump about two-thirds of the way down. At full tilt, this hump will really throw you. A couple of years ago, Mark's brother-in-law thought he would catch some air here and ended up catching a ride to the hospital in Minocqua. He broke two ribs. There is an alternate route just east of Suicide Hill for the more timid. Or the sane.

Even though it takes some driving to get here, it's worth every bit of the road fatigue, all the road grit, the highway blues. For a fine cup of joe or a sandwich for the trip home, check out Horhay's on the south end of Main in Minocqua.

Directions: From Woodruff take Highway 51 north to Highway 70, east to Highway 155, north through Sayner. West on Highway N three miles to McKay's Corner Store.

Fee: Donation for trail upkeep and maintenance on the new chalet. This system relies entirely on the efforts of volunteers and the generosity of users.

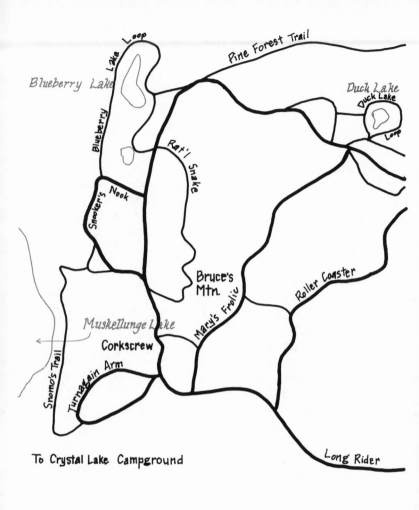

Blueberry Lake

Lake Loop

Pine Forest Trail

Duck Lake

Duck Lake Loop

Blueberry

Rat'l Snake

Snooker's Nook

Bruce's Mtn.

Mary's Frolic

Roller Coaster

Muskellunge Lake

Corkscrew

Snomo's Trail

Turnagain Arm

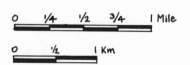

To Crystal Lake Campground

Long Rider

Parking   P

Mtn. Bike Trail ~

Single Track ~

N

0 1/4 1/2 3/4 1 Mile

0 1/2 1 Km

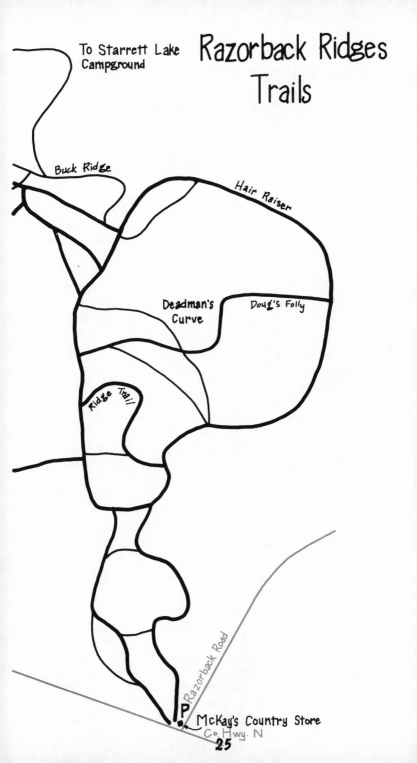

Rock Lake

The Rock Lake Trail probably sees more knobbies than any other trail in the 310 miles of the CAMBA system. The CAMBA trail network, all extremely well-mapped and well-marked, is simply the finest in the state. You could ride here for a month and still not see all the trails—trails that wind through thousands of acres of fine Northwoods country.

Rock Lake is the must-ride trail in a must-ride system, the first trail in the CAMBA system most riders check out. On weekends, a couple of dozen cars bearing Wisconsin, Minnesota, Iowa, and Illinois license plates choke the parking lot off County Highway M. The Rock Lake trails are also gaining notoriety with their inclusion into the Cable Classic mountain bike race because these trails are some of the most difficult in the race.

The 16-kilometer Rock Lake Loop, one of four loops in CAMBA's Namakagon Cluster, begins, along with the Glacier Loop, at the Forest Service parking lot. The Namakagon and Patsy Lake Loops start a couple of miles farther east on County M at the Namakagon Town Hall. Rock Lake is the most challenging trail in this cluster, although the Glacier Loop does have some tight singletrack—true singletrack, not the single path down a wide ski trail, like Rock Lake Loop. Most of the "singletrack" at Rock Lake is big ring stuff, singletrack laid out on doubletrack.

Rock Lake Loop, a narrow diagonal stride ski trail in winter, winds past some of the largest white and red pines next to any trail in Wisconsin. They're the size of trees you try to measure by reaching around. They make imposing guardrails. Two kilometers in, Rock Lake and Glacier Loops part company. Then at about three kilometers from the trailhead, a ski trail deviates from the main loop and circles Rock Lake. This trail, marked the Rock Lake Ski Trail, sports some soggy, mosquito-infested spots, but makeshift log bridges help passage. From this scenic trail, which traces the top of a ridge overlooking the lake, Rock Lake looked almost Bianchi-green at a certain angle on the misty and gray day we visited. The main loop skirts Hildebrand, Frels, and Birch Lakes two kilometers past Rock Lake, where we encountered hikers coming north to those lakes from a southern trailhead. A surprising number of hikers were enjoying the trail the day we rode, so be alert. Also be alert for horses; we saw evidence of their passing.

Just beyond Birch Lake, the trail makes an abrupt ascent, a granny-gear affair except for the strongest riders. The trail undulates the entire sixteen kilometers and momentum down the hills carries bike and rider up all but the toughest climbs—but not up this grunt of a climb. We found it easier, and a whole lot more challenging, to ride Rock Lake Loop at higher speeds. Big ringing the downhills, strewn with rocks and roots, will put the fear of God in all but the coolest riders. Slamming around Rock Lake Loop in the big ring isn't the way for most riders to enjoy the scenic nature of this trail, however. We actually preferred the slow loop, which we rode with the dogs.

Beyond the three lakes, the trail flattens somewhat and emerges from mostly white pine forest into maple and birch and eventually winds back to the parking lot. Ride this trail.

Directions: A Forest Service parking lot is seven miles east of Cable on County M, on the south side of the road. Lakewoods Resort is just east of Rock Lake on County M, and there are numerous National Forest campgrounds in the area, such as Day Lake and East Twin Lake to the southeast.

Fee: There is a $3 parking fee. We suggest either joining CAMBA or purchasing a complete set of their excellent maps. Contact CAMBA, P.O. Box 141, Cable, Wisconsin 54821 Telephone is 800-533-7454 and website is www.cable4fun. com/camba.

Rock Lake Trails

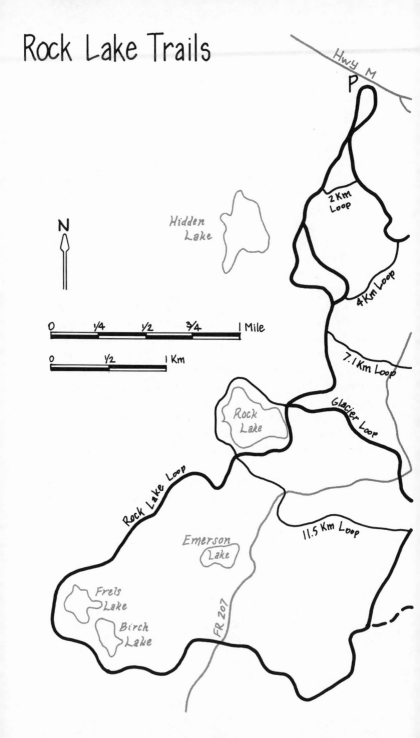

Hwy M

FR 207

Glacier Loop

Rock Lake Loop

7.1 Km Loop

Parking   P
Mtn. Bike Trail ∼

Glacier Loop

Pines & Mines ★

★ Rock Lake

Fat Tire 40 ★

Razorback Ridges ★

★ Escanaba

★ Anvil & Nicolet
North

McNaughton Trail ★

The Northern Shorts

The Blue Hills

The ski trails at Bruce climb up and into the Blue Hills. A cross-country ski race, held each January on these trails, is aptly named the Blue Hills Ascent. Some of the climbs here ascend as much as three hundred feet, so be prepared to grind away on the doubletrack ski trail. A couple of the descents have some tricky turns and low spots. These low, soggy spots are the worst aspect of a trail system that offers some stunning views of the famed Blue Hills.

Directions: Take Highway 40 north from Highway 8 near Bruce to County Highway O. Then head west on County O six miles to Fire Lane Road. Go north on Fire Lane Road one mile; trails are on the right. For information contact www.centuryinter.net /bluehills.

CAMBA

If we could ride just one place in Wisconsin, that would be CAMBA, the Chequamegon Area Mountain Bike Association's network of trails. Three hundred plus miles of trail through some of the finest country in the state—the Namekagon River Valley, the Birkie Highlands, the Rock Lake Kettle Moraine, and the Great Divide region. You'll have to drive over a thousand miles to find a better system.

This book includes maps of two of the better known CAMBA trails: Rock Lake and the Chequamegon Fat Tire 40 course. Many other challenging trails await, including the Frost Pocket Loop, the Esker Trail, the Drummond Ski Trails, and the North Country Trail.

The 6.7-mile Frost Pocket Loop starts at the Birkie Warming Hut on County Highway OO, goes west on OO to Phipps Fire Lane, then south on Phipps to Snowmobile Trail 5 to Snowmobile Trail 8, which eventually intersects Old OO. Old OO runs west to the sprawling metropolis of Seeley or east back to the warming hut. This doubletrack loop, part of the Northwest Series' Seeley Lions Club Pre-Fat race, runs up and down some tough hills, here courtesy of the last glacier.

Additionally, some nifty singletrack loops through the massive white pines in the Uhrenholdt State Forest (named after Sigurd Olson's father-in-law) off County OO and through the Seeley Ski Trails off Old County OO. Just north of Seeley on Highway 63 sits Silverthorn Lake, another trailhead which also features a small beach for swimming. Occasionally, the Chequama Mamas (pronounced like shuwama mama) take their weekly Thursday night rides from here or the Birkie warming hut.

Starting on Spider Lake Road, the Esker Trail is a 6.7-mile loop which intersects the road to Telemark Lodge a kilometer south of Highway M. Singletrack runs into the woods shortly after this intersection. This trail climbs up onto the back of an esker and rides it southeast. The trail winds past Island Lake and picks up the Bill Koch Ski Trail, which makes its way back to Spider Lake Road. The Telemark Trails, and all the gut-wrenching climbs, lie close-by at the lodge.

Riders can get to the Drummond Ski Trails from either the Drummond Town Park on the shores of Lake Drummond or the Drummond Ski Trails parking lot, which means a three dollar user fee for the Forest Service. We started at the park, picking up a CAMBA map, and rode the mile or so on pavement to the trailhead.

The main trail here is Boulevard, an eight-mile out and back ride from Drummond, turning around at the Lake Owen Picnic Area. This is an ideal ride for a sultry July or August day—pack a towel and swimming trunks, a lunch if there's room, ride to the lake, go for a swim, and ride back.

The trails cover sharp terrain, reminding us of the hills at Razorback, and the trail surface sucked at our tires. Boulevard, along with Jack Rabbit and Antler Trails which spur off Boulevard, are wide ski trails, similar to those at Rock Lake, and shouldn't present any scares.

The North Country Trail offered more technical riding and lots of dismounting over dozens of trees still across the trail. The area was hit with two windstorms in July of 1999, the first the same one that ripped through the Boundary Waters. Although mainly a hiking trail, the North Country winds to the west/northwest through the Delta and Drummond clusters. It crosses Highway 63 a mile east of Drummond and meanders up toward Cisco, Overby, Esox, and Bullhead Lakes before entering the Rainbow Lake Wilderness, where bicycles are prohibited.

For food and drink, check out the Black Bear or

Chequamegon Saloons in Drummond. Both are right on Highway 63.

There are dozens more trails in the CAMBA system. For more information or a complete set of finely detailed maps contact CAMBA, P.O. Box 141, Cable, Wisconsin 54821. Website is camba@cheqnet.net or www.cable4fun.com/camba and telephone is 800-533-7454.

Copper Falls State Park

Most folks who mountain bike in the Mellen area ride at Copper Falls State Park, which is definitely worth checking out, especially for waterfall connoisseurs. It features three falls, all on the Bad River as it makes its headlong rush to Lake Superior, including park namesake Copper Falls. Unfortunately, riders can pedal only to Red Granite Falls. Copper and Brownstone Falls lie along hiking-only trails, but both are worth walking to. It's nice to get off and stretch a bit anyway.

Directions: Two miles northeast of Mellen off Highway 169.

Deep Lake Trails-Vilas County Forest

These trails are a tangled web of town roads and logging roads, portions of which are also snowmobile trails. Shortly before we rode them, ATV vandals had pulled all the trail markers, so we can't comment on how well things are marked. Without markers it definitely takes some concentration and a map to navigate the area without getting lost.

We encountered lots of loose sand, both on town road sections and logging roads. If you get off on the feel of a bike snaking out of control in dune-like sand, you'll love these trails. Another exotic experience we had was cranking both small rings because of the deep sand, while still getting our teeth jarred by road corduroy. Should be impossible, but . . .

While most of the trails wind through big clear-cut patches of forest (an ice storm damaged many of the jack pine a few years ago, and that was used as an excuse by the professional foresters for whacking everything), there is a lovely little remote park at the confluence of Buckatabon Creek and the Wisconsin River. A fire ring and picnic shelter invite a repast. Bring some food.

Directions: From Eagle River take Highway 45 north three miles to County Highway G. Go left on G one and a quarter miles to Croker Road. Turn right on Croker and drive until you see the Hunter Lake Recreation Area sign. Follow the signs until you reach the lake, which has a nice beach. Park at the beach and start riding.

East Twin Lake

We thought about calling this ride the ELF Loop, but opted for the more geographical name of East Twin Lake, the Chequamegon National Forest campground where this ride begins. We considered ELF Loop because the first part of the ride runs by the ELF (Extremely Low Frequency) lines, a communication system used by the Navy to reach nuclear submarines at sea. Now that the Cold War is over some Americans consider the system obsolete and protest annually in the Clam Lake area.

Our loop begins at East Twin Lake, which offers ten campsites, one a walk-in. The lake is also home to several loons who laugh and call most of the night. The loop circles around the lake on Forest Roads 193 and 195, and then turns due east on FR 182 and shortly crosses the ELF lines. The Forest Service dumps coarse gravel, lots of it, on most of their roads, and 182 is no exception, so wide knobbies, like 2.1" tires, are a must.

Forest Road 182 runs straight east through low, swampy land that's home to Wisconsin's recently reintroduced elk herd. One reason the elk were introduced in the Clam Lake area was so they could take advantage of the mowed open meadows along the miles of ELF lines. Wolf packs also roam this remote area. After six miles on FR 182, turn left on FR 183, which travels northwest into higher country toward the Gogebic Range, and crosses the McCarthy Creek drainage. Another six miles and FR 183 runs into FR 184, which shortly intersects County GG. We rode on these wide Forest Service gravel roads for over an hour without meeting a soul, unless we count the five deer encountered along the way. For those seeking more technical riding numerous walking trails and doubletrack veer into the woods for incalculable variations of this loop. One of these unmarked doubletracks climbs a windy maple ridge to the Marengo Fire Tower and its view north toward Lake Superior.

Highway GG runs generally southwest to East Twin Lake. Take this asphalt road left back to the campground for a twenty-three-mile ride. For a longer loop, take a right on FR 196 after riding GG south a mile and a half. This road bears west over the Brunsweiler River, intersecting FR 344 in four miles and FR 194 in six. Both of these roads run south, or left, back to FR 193, which rolls back to East Twin Lake. The ride all the way over to FR 194 ends up being over thirty miles, much of this through deep gravel. Bring food, water, spare tubes and tools—you're literally in the sticks here.

Once again, there are endless options and multiple loops. See the USGS map of the Hayward, Washburn, and Glidden Ranger Districts of the Chequamegon National Forest, available at the district headquarters or the Heart of the Chequamegon convenience store in Clam Lake. This map is invaluable for mountain bikers who want to ride the hundreds of miles in the Chequamegon.

Flambeau River State Forest

The DNR boasts of over one hundred miles of ridable cross-country ski trails, ATV trails, and logging roads in this section of state forest. The Oxbo Ski Trails run north along the Flambeau River, starting along Highway 70 at the cross-country trailhead 15 miles west of Fifield. This doubletrack is best in spring and fall. In summer, the grass along the trail grows water-bottle-high, and the black flies are vicious. Low, swampy, bug-infested terrain finally ended our ride here. We also tried starting from the southern lot on County Highway W, just east of the river and past the well-maintained DNR cabin on the shores of the Flambeau River (bring the canoe). This section was also grassy and swampy. For summer riding here, take the ATV trails or the gravel roads in the state forest. These see heavy traffic, which consequently knocks the grass down. Snuss Boulevard, one of the many roads here, connects the northern ski trails with the southern trails.

Directions: The northern parking lot is located on Highway 70 near Oxbo on the Flambeau River, six miles east of the Loretta-Draper Metroplex. The southern parking lot is east of the river on County W, sixteen miles west of Phillips.

Lauterman Trail

Nine miles of mostly doubletrack and logging roads form three loops in this remote location in the Nicolet National Forest. If Lauterman wasn't so far from civilization, these rolling trails would see much more use. On the other hand, being in the middle of nowhere means no other mountain bikers most times, which these days isn't such a bad thing.

Don't expect technical riding at Lauterman. The Forest Service, like the state forest managers, likes to be able to patrol and maintain trail by truck, which leads to wide serviceable trail. The steepest hills remain the most challenging element here.

The Forest Service operates several campgrounds within riding distance (a five-mile radius) of the Lauterman trailhead. The Perch Lake campground is north of Highway 70, while the Lauterman Lake campground is closest to the trailhead on FR 2154. The Lost Lake and Chipmunk Rapids campgrounds are farther to the southwest on FR 2156. Take a weekend, camp and ride.

For information contact the Eagle River Ranger District, P.O. Box 1809, Eagle River, Wisconsin 54521. Telephone is 715-479-2827.

Directions: The Lauterman Trail is twelve miles west of Florence off Highway 70. Turn left, or south, off 70 onto FR 2154. The trailhead and parking lot lie a quarter mile down FR 2154 on the right side. Coming from the west, the trailhead is approximately forty miles east of Eagle River.

Lumberjack Trail

This trail is an amalgamation of an old diagonal ski trail, the Lumberjack, and some snowmobile trails, put together by the Boulder Area Trail System (BATS). Some of the snowmobile trail is wide logging road. There's no technical singletrack, but the quarter mile down to Fishtrap Dam is narrow and moderately challenging. The section from the wooden bridge across White Sand Creek to Old Highway K is also fun: a fast, pine needle cushioned path between big pines.

This ride begins behind the Chamber of Commerce building, where the trail heads west off the blacktop bike trail.

Circle around the baseball field to center field, where the trail veers right into the woods. Here, and elsewhere along the trail, look for the colored square signs with an arrow and the BATS logo. If you can't figure what the logo would be, here's a hint: it's a drawing of a creature that uses sonar for navigation.

Lots of pine cones decorate the sandy trail, along with myriad deer prints. About the time you've settled into your pedals you'll hit an intersection strewn with signs. We counted eleven signposts. Find the BATS sign and head left. Soon you'll cross Old Highway K and reenter the woods going due east. This section of trail is an old (very old, given the eighteen-inch-diameter pines along the embankments on either side) railroad grade used in the early logging days.

You'll briefly join another road, Conora, negotiate between a couple of boulders placed there to block motorized vehicles, and ride near the north shore of White Sand Lake. No Name Lake will be visible on the left, then you'll get an even better view of Nellie Lake on the right. After passing two more big rocks, bare left and ride around the chain gate that marks the beginning of the Lumberjack Trail section of this ride.

For the first time, you'll be negotiating a less graded, more bumpy, less groomed, more grassy trail. It's a mild roller coaster for about three miles, without much scenery but enough downhill loose sand to keep you interested.

Go right at the next junction, where a sign points to Fishtrap Dam. The dam, which is an iron bar and concrete affair, is only a couple of feet high, creating a sprawling, lilly-pad-choked pond. Bald eagles frequent the area. So do deer flies. Below the dam, the Manitowish River continues west toward its confluence with the Turtle River and the Turtle-Flambeau Flowage.

From the dam, re-ride the dam trail and take either of two loops until you reach the Wooden Bridge across White Sand Creek. There's a climb on the other side of the creek. Take the right path and avoid causing erosion problems on the steep hill straight ahead. At the top of the hill, bear right into the pine woods and ride the cushy carpet of pine needles until you reach Old Highway K again. The trail crosses the road and drops down to just north of where all those signs were on your way out. Turn right at this next junction and it's a short ride back to the ball diamond.

Directions: From the corner of Highways K and M in downtown Boulder Junction, take M south three-fourths of a mile to the Chamber of Commerce office on the left. Park at the baseball field behind the Chamber office. For information contact the Boulder Junction Chamber of Commerce, P.O. Box 286, Boulder Junction, Wisconsin 54512. Website is www.boulderjct.org and telephone is 800-466-8759.

Fee: The BATS does not charge a fee. There is a $3 daily/$10 annual trail fee for DNR trails.

Madeline

Madeline is truly a lady. Her ten miles of trail are well-behaved doubletrack logging roads that loop gently through both young (logged in the early 1980s) and old forest. The old stuff is on the east side of the trail, nearest to Madeline Lake. Many white and red pine measure over six feet in circumference. The trail's design, an outside loop with three inside connecting loops, offers a choice among four different lengths of ride.

An interesting detour spurs off the trail and up Madeline Lake Road. Although paved, the road has some quick little hills and sharp turns. About a half mile from the trail, another unmarked, paved road heads off to the left, or east. To the south of this road is the Woodruff State Fish Hatchery. But don't bother bringing your fishing pole; there's a tall fence. Only the gulls get lunch.

If you follow this unmarked road east for a quarter mile, it ends at a boat launching ramp. Make the steep climb onto a little knob of land that forms a peninsula out into Madeline Lake. There's a short but neat little piece of singletrack here.

For information contact the DNR Office, 4125 County Highway M, Boulder Junction, Wisconsin 54512. Telephone is 715-385-2727.

Directions: From the intersection of Highway 47 and County Highway J, head east on J one mile, then go north on Rudolph Road a mile and a quarter to a parking lot on the right.

Minocqua Winter Park

Thirty kilometers of doubletrack ski trails crisscross Winter Park. A difficult section of trail climbs up to the Squirrel Hill Lookout and a beautiful view of the surrounding area. Try the hair-raising singletrack descent on the west side of the hill, a straight shot down. Most riders, all except those with exceptional descending skills, should climb up the singletrack and descend the service road. The aptly named VO2 Max Trail climbs and descends the second tallest hill in the area. The newest ski trail out to Lake Marie travels through some interesting terrain, and past some bald eagles. There always seems to be an eagle or two flying around this area. The ski area does have some low places. Stay away from Island Hop Trail. Miles of gravel roads in the area are worth exploring, too, especially to the south toward the Willow Flowage.

Directions: From the intersection of Highways 51 and 70 in Woodruff, take Highway 70 west six miles to Squirrel Lake Road. Go south six miles on Squirrel Lake Road to Scotchman Lake Road, then left and follow the signs to Winter Park. Look for the fire tower on Squirrel Hill.

Mount Ashwabay

After thirty-two seasons as owner and manager of Mount Ashwabay near Bayfield, Jerry Carlson has seen just about everything, except a lot of mountain bikers. According to Jerry, only a couple dozen riders a week try out the Ashwabay trails. Seems a shame. With over sixteen miles of trail and some impressive terrain, Ashwabay is versatile. A downhill and cross-country ski area in the winter, the trails are not mowed in the summer. Except for Deer Path, which skirts the south side of the mountain, most get just enough use to keep the weeds at bay.

Jerry asks that ATBers stay off the downhill slopes to prevent erosion. For a tough climb, try Swiss Miss. Find it by heading out Sugar Bush from the ski chalet. Swiss Miss heads off to the left and up the hill a couple hundred yards down Sugar Bush. Sugar Bush Trail continues and passes an old cabin, used by the local landowners for making maple syrup in the spring. For information contact Mount Ashwabay at P.O. Box 928, Bayfield, Wisconsin 54814. Telephone is 715-779-3227.

Directions: From Bayfield go south three miles to Ski Hill Road. Turn right and continue one mile, up an impressive hill, to where the road dead ends at the ski hill.

Newman Springs

With only slightly over seven miles of trail, Newman Springs in the Park Falls District of the Chequamegon National Forest is too little of a good thing. Trails A and B loop left out of the parking area, near the sign board. Loop E begins farther back in the parking area, near an old sand pit. All trails begin as roads, but don't fret, they narrow out a bit and get full of skin-ripping raspberries soon enough. Loop B is accessible from A. Loops C and D are ski trails and, unless you have flotation in addition to suspension, way too wet for riding.

Loops A and B offer the most diversity, including several steep climbs and descents, a spring-fed pond full of trout (we didn't fish, but it looked like a good spot), and about fifty yards of bog riding—okay after a dry summer, maybe impassable during a wet one. Loop B provides a brief but glorious ride through a dense hemlock woods on a north-facing slope.

Loop E is longer, about four miles, and also takes you by a trout pond and the diminutive Penny Lake. It also makes a couple of creek crossings on plank bridges and passes within handlebar distance of two giant white spruce, thirty inches in diameter.

Oh, and watch out for a gaping hole in the middle of the trail near the spruce. We didn't see it soon enough and went ass over handlebar.

Directions: From Park Falls and Highway 13 take Highway 182 east twelve miles to the parking area on the right. For information contact the USDA Forest Service, 1170 South Fourth Avenue, Park Falls, Wisconsin 54552. Telephone is 715-762-2461.

The North Country Trail

The North Country Trail, a National Scenic Trail like the Ice Age Trail, slices through the Copper Falls State Park. A good chunk of the ridable trails in the park run concurrently with the North Country Trail. This trail starts in the Adirondacks of upstate New York and meanders west to North Dakota. The bulk of the North Country Trail crosses the most northern tier of Wisconsin counties—Douglas, Bayfield, Ashland, Iron—in the Chequamegon National Forest. This trail was originally planned as a hiking trail, but multi-use (read mountain biking) is allowable in many sections. Ride where not posted against mountain biking.

Two of the better jumping-off spots lie between Mellen and Clam Lake off County GG. Start at either Lake Three or Beaver Lake, both national forest campgrounds. The North Country Trail travels both east and west from either spot, following blue blaze marks. This singletrack trail crosses hundreds of logging roads and forest roads on its way across the state, extending nearly limitless riding possibilities. Riders comfortable with their orienteering skills will appreciate the many options. For those not so sure of how to get around the woods, stay with the blue blazes. ATBers can also pick up the North Country Trail north of Cable near the CAMBA trails.

The North Country is one of the most technical trails in the Chequamegon. East of Lake Three the trail gets rocky and suspension helped out immensely. We started to slip on the rocks after a brief shower.

Directions: Lake Three is eight miles east of Mellen on County GG. Take FR 187 right, or north. This splits to the left at a junction with FR 188, or Hanson Road. Cross the Brunsweiler River (watch for a natural spring on the left side of the road as you approach the river) and continue to Pine Stump Corner (check out an interesting sign here explaining the place-name). Forest Road 187 turns right, or north, here and Lake Three is just a mile down the road. The North Country Trail intersects FR 187 before the campground. Beaver Lake lies southwest of Lake Three. Follow the directions to Lake Three. At Pine Stump Corner, continue west on FR 198. Turn right at the intersection of FR 387, or Clam Lake Road. We recommend a *Wisconsin Atlas and Gazetteer* or USGS maps and a compass if riding the North Country Trail.

Phillips

This cross-country ski area offers six miles of doubletrack ski trail through immature woods, along with a growing amount of singletrack blazed each year by the local club. Although not the most scenic or smoothest ride in the area, it is convenient, sitting right off Highway 13. It's a place to stop and ride on the way to and from more northern destinations. Several short steep descents and sandy climbs punctuate the Phillips course, which is one reason why the Dirtfighter, a Wisconsin Off-Road Series race, is held here in July. Some of the single-track also takes advantage of what vertical is here. Most of these climbs require the granny-gear and maybe some pushing. Ride four or five laps and you'll get a punishing aerobic workout.

While in Phillips visit two historical landmarks: Concrete Park and the Crystal Cafe. Concrete Park, home of the best grotto sculptures in Wisconsin, lies a mile south of Phillips on Highway 13. Check out the giant muskie behind the big oak in the middle of the park. It's better than the one at the Fishing Hall of Fame in Hayward. The Crystal Cafe simply has some of the best pie in the Northwoods, rivaling that other Crystal Cafe in Iola. Find it on the west side of Main Street.

Directions: Trails lie on the north side of town. Park at the huge Marquip building on the east side of Highway 13. A gravel road winds east and north, intersecting the trail system a mile from the parking lot. The trails are poorly marked, but all the loops are closed, hemmed in by Duroy Lake and Squaw Creek, so it's difficult to get lost.

Raven Trail

Located near Woodruff in the American Legion-Northern Highlands State Forest, the Raven has a reputation among cross-country skiers as a bone breaker. Actually, there are only a couple of really difficult hills at Raven, and these are all on the outside Expert Loop. Riders can enjoy views of Clear and Hemlock Lakes by cruising this loop, but be careful, especially when making the choice about bypassing a difficult hill near Hemlock Lake. The downhill is steep and full of loose gravel, with a few bigger rocks thrown in for fun. It's a difficult ride down.

There's a short, one-mile nature trail that makes for an informative ride. One of our favorite sections of this trail is after the big hill, along the shores of Hemlock Lake. The trail goes through a wonderful hemlock woods, where the sun never shines directly on the ground.

With eleven miles of lovely, and sometimes tricky trail, dull is a feeling you'll get nevermore at Raven.

Directions: From the intersection of Highway 47 and County Highway J go two miles east on Highway 47 to Woodruff Road. Turn left on Woodruff Road and continue a half mile south to a parking lot on the right.

Sisters Farm

Just west of Ladysmith, the Sisters Farm Ski Trails, groomed for diagonal striding in winter, start and wind through mild terrain along the Flambeau River. Although Sisters Farm (home of a Wisconsin Off-Road Series [WORS] race) has no numbing climbs, some of the singletrack is the most root- and rock-infested trail in the entire state, and quite numbing in its own way. Suspension or low tire pressure helps smooth the many jolts. All totaled the single and doubletrack covers five miles, and this lack of distance is the most negative feature of Sisters Farm.

Directions: From Highway 27, turn west on Port Arthur Road and go past Mount Senario College and two miles to Sisters Farm Road. The trails are on the west side of the road.

VAMBASA

Like CAMBA, VAMBASA (the Vilas Area Mountain Bike and Ski Association) has linked and mapped individual trail systems within a given area. Vilas County, with its numerous lakes that cover nearly one third of the county land mass, is arguably the most scenic county in the state. Couple this with ample public land, most of it state forest, and we have a recipe for some stunning mountain biking.

Razorback Ridges outside of Sayner is one of the top three places in the state to ride, or cross-country ski for that matter. Just to the north of Razorback lies Escanaba Lake. The Anvil Trail in the extreme southeast corner of the county is also part of VAMBASA. Nine other lesser-known trails round out the system, a network which easily totals over one

hundred miles. Previously we highlighted two of these nine—
Deep Lake Trails (page 34) and Lumberjack Trail (page 37).
For a map contact VAMBASA, P.O. Box 189, Arbor Vitae,
Wisconsin 54568 or www.vilas.com.

Washburn Lake

This is one of those hidden gems that only the locals seem to
know about. In fact, if this section of the Oneida County
Forest had more miles, it would be one of the more popular
trail systems in the state. Then everybody would know about
it, so it's just as well with only seven miles of trail.

Basically, Washburn Lake is one clockwise 4.2-mile doubletrack loop that traverses some sharp glacial ridges and
valleys. In winter, it's the place for Rhinelander's cross-country skiers to ski. This loop in itself is challenging enough, and
all but the strongest riders will need the granny-gear to make
the toughest climbs.

The singletrack, however, is what drew us to this trail
system. It is some of the nicest singletrack in the state; it's too
bad there's only 2.8 miles of it. These narrow trails meander
up and down the ridges, around aspen and oak trees, and over
stones and roots. This singletrack, much of it built by local
rider Dennis Loy, also requires a small gear and large lungs.

The trails aren't marked, but they're simple to find. And
there's a detailed mapboard at the trailhead and smaller maps
for trail use. All of the loops run clockwise.

Directions: Washburn Lake is approximately six miles west
of Rhinelander off Highway 8. Take County Highway N
north through the metropolis of Woodboro about a half mile.
Turn left, or west, on Washburn Lake Road and go a little
over a mile. The trailhead is on the right, or north, side of the
road. For information contact Oneida County Forest at P.O.
Box 400, Courthouse, Rhinelander, Wisconsin 54501.
Telephone is 715-369-6140.

Fee: Donations are requested and can be placed in the drop
box at the trailhead.

Otter Lake ● ●Harrison Hills

Medford
District ●

New
Wood

Jack
Lake ● ●Crocker Hills

●Bear Paw Inn

Lake Wissota ●

Big Eau Pleine ● ●Berkhahn
Rookery
●Green Circle

Tigerton ●

Brown County●
Reforestation

●Baird Creek

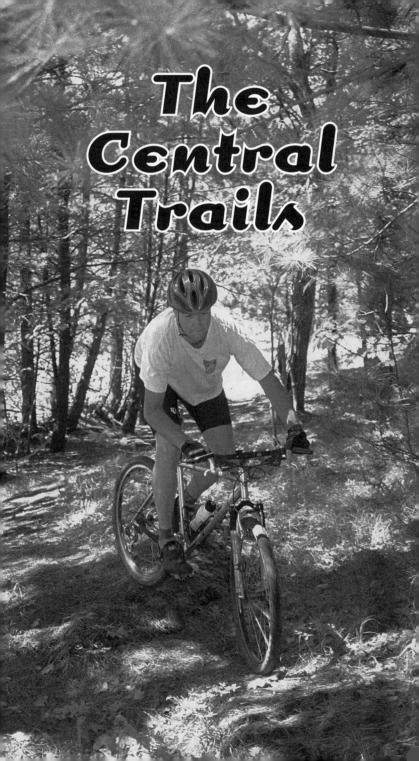

The Central Trails

Newport State Park

The sounds of clicking gears and pounding surf are not something most Wisconsin ATB riders have heard while riding the state's trails. But riders at Newport State Park can not only hear this unusual combination of sounds; if they ride there on a day when wind is really whipping from the east, they can even get wet.

The DNR established Newport in 1964. It has a rich history, dating back to the early 1800s, and several park publications tell its story well. The park is managed "as if it were a wilderness area," which means there are no drive-to campgrounds. The fifteen campsites are located along the hiking/skiing/biking path, some less than a mile from the nearest parking lot, some over two.

There are roughly twenty miles of developed trail at Newport, but Fern, Ridge, Sand Cove, Duck Bay, Meadow, and part of Europe Bay Trails are closed to biking. While this sounds like a lot, these comprise less than twenty-five percent of the system's mileage.

A trip out Newport Trail to Varney Point covers five miles. The terrain is mostly tame. Much of the trail is wide, flat, and smooth hardpack. Lake Michigan is never too far away and an excursion to its shore is worthwhile. Ducks sit on the water when it's calm enough, cormorants dive for fish, and the ubiquitous gulls look for scraps. One prominent feature, visible anywhere from the southeast shore, is Spider Island. This flat, sprawling landform reminds some of a desert island sans palm trees. It's a testament to the lake's fury that nothing on the island stands more than a few feet high.

The forest along the Newport Trail is unique for several reasons. One of the most frequently seen trees is white cedar. These trees are common only in low, swampy areas most places in Wisconsin, but they grow all over the northern

Door Peninsula. Some here are quite large. Another tree uncommon in most of the state is the American beech. It's recognizable by its very smooth gray-blue bark.

There are seven campsites along the Newport Trail, all on the Lake Michigan side. The paths to them make interesting, if short, side trips. These also go closer to the lake. Each site has a rustic bench and a fire pit with grill. Some have outhouses with pit toilets not far away. Near campsite number 10, the Newport Trail takes a hard right and heads back overland to the parking lot. The trail straight ahead is called the Rowleys Bay Trail, traveling as it does near the shore of Rowleys Bay. We jogged this section of trail because we didn't want to get pounded by bumps. The trail is narrow, winds between cedar, and is crisscrossed with tree roots, mostly cedar. Farther down, as it turns inland away from the lake, dolomite rock ledges add more fun, or pain.

The short Pine Loop cuts through a pine plantation and ends at parking area one, near the entrance to the park. Stay on Rowleys Bay Trail to get back to parking areas two and three.

Parking area three is the site of the former village of Newport, which flourished during the late 1800s. A privately owned pier jutted out into the lake, from which thousands of cords of logs were shipped south. The beach east of this parking area is sandy and clean, free of rocks. It's an inviting place for a swim if the day is nice and water is warm.

The Europe Bay Trail extends northward, though not as immediately close to Lake Michigan as the southern trails. It does provide a couple of views of Europe Lake, one of the few small lakes on the peninsula.

Directions: From Ellison Bay take Highway 42 three miles to County Highway NP, turn right, and follow the signs to the park entrance. For information contact Newport State Park, 475 County Highway NP, Ellison Bay, Wisconsin 54210. Telephone is 920-854-2500.

Fee: A Wisconsin Parks vehicle sticker and a trail pass are required.

Newport State Park Trails

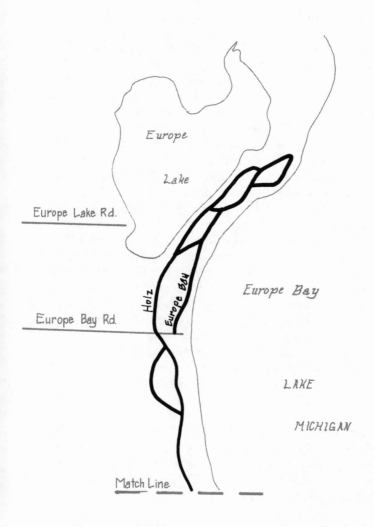

Europe Lake

Europe Lake Rd.

Holz

Europe Bay

Europe Bay

Europe Bay Rd.

LAKE

MICHIGAN

Match Line

Parking   P

Mtn. Bike Trail   ~

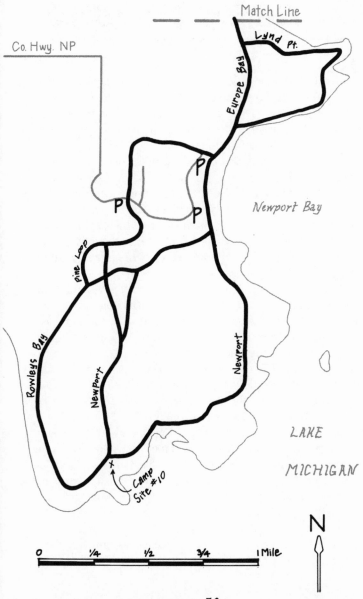

Match Line

Co. Hwy. NP

Lynd Pt.

Europe Bay

Newport Bay

P

P

P

Pine Loop

Rowleys Bay

Newport

Newport

Camp Site #10

x

LAKE

MICHIGAN

0   ¼   ½   ¾   1 Mile

N

Nine Mile County Forest

For off-roaders who live in the Wausau area, Nine Mile County Forest is the place to ride. Few trail systems in north central Wisconsin have the variety of terrain or the length and type of trails found here. Arguably, it's one of the top mountain bike destinations in the state.

For years, a local group of dedicated riders, led by the indefatigable Les Schwartz, has developed an extensive network of singletrack at Nine Mile to go along with the thirty kilometers of cross-country ski trail. This mix of trail satisfies beginner and expert alike. All of the ski trail is clearly marked, with laminated maps posted at the major intersections. In the spring of 2000, much of the singletrack was marked, ending much of the confusion of riders new to the area.

Much of the singletrack, which started as a walking trail between targets for a national archery tournament, sits inside the inner ski loops. Simply ride down Trail P, the main ski trail leading away from the chalet, turn right, and start looking for singletrack into the pine and birch trees. Singletrack 5, marked by a small blue number, meanders back and forth, crisscrossing the ski trail at several points.

Some of the best (most technical) singletrack lies east of Red Bud Road (the main road through Nine Mile) off Leo's Loop, or Trail C. Just across Red Bud, Singletrack 3 heads north off Trail C and another section winds south. These both eventually come back to Trail C. Farther down Trail C, Singletracks 1 and 2 veer off and eventually back onto the main ski trail. Singletracks 1 and 3 offer the most technical riding. Riding the rock gardens on 1 and 3 cleanly, especially the boulders on 1, is an accomplishment. Even today, we find ourselves bouncing off a stubborn chunk of granite and tumbling or sliding out on an exposed root.

Our favorite section of singletrack sits on the west side of Red Bud and starts with a left at the base of the second climb on Trail D (affectionately called Bitch Two by local riders and skiers). Called the Ho Chi Minh Trail, Singletrack 8 climbs a high ridge. At the top—Rib Mountain rising beyond the maple and oak ridges—granite rocks litter the trail and pummel both bike and rider until the trail exits on Trail I.

Singletrack 9—dubbed the Flower Trail because of the thousands of trilliums, dog-tooth violets, and bloodroot that carpet the surrounding woods in April and May—enters and exits off the snowmobile trail along the western edge of Nine Mile. It's difficult to get handlebars past the tightly spaced popples along this trail and occasionally a ruffed grouse flushes here.

For those who seek milder riding, doubletrack ski trail winds throughout the 4,900 acres of county land. Trails L and LL, the newest and most difficult sections of ski trail built at the request of skiers who felt Nine Mile was too tame, tackle the highest ridge in the forest. These are the most difficult ski trails. Watch out for the rocky, tire-slashing drainage ditches across the trail on the sharp descents. Trail I, the Bushwacker, takes the most southern loop in the forest and also tackles some impressive hardwood ridges.

The best way to learn the Nine Mile mountain bike trails is to ride with those who know the trails. Every Thursday evening during the season, group rides, divided into three ability levels, leave the main parking lot. Experienced riders lead each group, so this ride is an excellent way to learn Nine Mile's singletrack—as well as meet new riders.

There are other trails around the Nine Mile area, so ask local riders about trails south of Nine Mile through the Wausau and Mosinee School Forests and those up and around nearby Rib Mountain.

For information contact the Marathon County Forestry Department, 500 Forest Street, Wausau, Wisconsin 54403. Telephone is 715-261-1580 or 715-693-3001.

Directions: From Highway 51 at County Highway N, go four miles west on County N to Red Bud Road. Go left on Red Bud and the parking lot is a mile and a half south on the right.

Fee: Yearly passes are available through the county forest office. Daily fees are payable at a box at the trailhead.

Nine Mile County Forest Trails

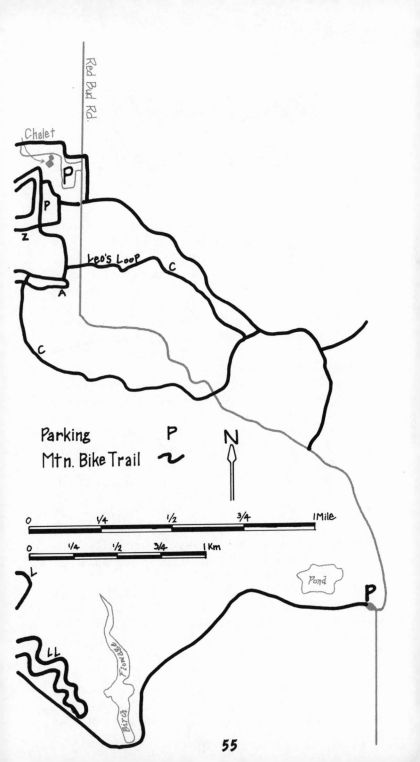

Red Bud Rd.

Chalet

P

P

Z

Leo's Loop

C

A

C

Parking   P

Mtn. Bike Trail ∿

N

| 0 | 1/4 | 1/2 | 3/4 | 1 Mile |

| 0 | 1/4 | 1/2 | 3/4 | 1 Km |

L

Pond

P

LL

Flower

Birch

Peninsula State Park

Peninsula State Park is definitely a maritime experience. It smells like it. Sounds like it, looks like it, feels like it. While riding either the crushed limestone bike trail along the shore or the mountain bike trails in the interior of the park, we could smell the bay. Gulls flew overhead or screeched and fought for food. We caught the glistening bay in glimpses through the dense white cedars. One of the few things that didn't seem maritime was the presence of yellow lady slippers growing quietly among the cedars and maples. They have a distinctly Northwoods feeling.

The park, just north of the quaint village of Fish Creek, doesn't offer technically challenging trails. Come expecting easy to moderate trails, as well as things that Door County is known for—beaches and summer fun, nineteenth-century architecture and views of the bay and lake, cherries and apples, and cool weather.

The Sunset Bike Trail, a 5.1-mile crushed limestone trail, cruises the edge of the northern-most finger of the park. Besides Sunset, the park offers seven miles of what the DNR calls rough terrain, singletrack trail on cross-country ski trails. Interestingly, the DNR doesn't charge for the highly developed bike trail but requires a state trail pass for the minimally maintained "rough terrain" trails. Go figure.

Sunset Bike Trail hugs the shoreline. Across the bay, the shores of Michigan's Upper Peninsula stretch northward toward Escanaba. Sailboats on pleasure cruises and freighters headed to port at Green Bay ply the tricky waters. Porte des Morts Passage (Death's Door) stands between the peninsula proper and Washington Island. The fishy aroma that comes with all big water blows ashore. Yes, it's a maritime experience.

A third of the way up Sunset Trail, Eagle Bluff Lighthouse guards the bay. This structure, built in 1868 of Cream City

Brick, is now a museum, complete with guided tours.

Peninsula is a busy park in summer, catering to those who prefer industrial tourism. Visit in early spring before green-up or late fall after the leaves have fallen. Besides the RVers, Peninsula does see hundreds of bicyclists, of all varieties. On the crushed limestone trail, we saw many riders on single and three speeds. Mom, Dad, Grandpa, Grandma, and the Kids. This was encouraging. Peninsula caters to family riding.

One reason to visit at the height of the tourist season is the refrigerator effect of the big water. No matter which way the wind is blowing, it comes off the bay or the lake. In other words, Peninsula is one cool place, about ten degrees cooler than the rest of the state. The day we visited, the rest of the state simmered in ninety-degree heat. We, however, felt comfortable.

The mountain bike trails (cross-country ski trails) offer moderate challenge. The only hill in the system comes right after the turn from Sunset onto the "Off-Road Bike Trail." This hill can be fun to careen down on the return trip if you ride it hard in the big ring. The rest of the trails run through dense woods, often white cedar, never really changing altitude. Ridden hard, they can offer some challenge.

Walk around the village of Fish Creek before leaving. Some of the original architecture still stands—for instance, the Church of Atonement, tucked away in cedars. Rental bikes are available at the park entrance and at Nor Door Sport & Cyclery.

Directions: Take Highway 42 north through Fish Creek to a large state park sign on the left. Turn left and the park entrance is just ahead. For information contact Peninsula State Park, Box 218, Fish Creek, Wisconsin, 54234. Telephone is 920-868-3258.

Fee: A Wisconsin Parks vehicle sticker and a trail pass are required.

Peninsula State Park Trails

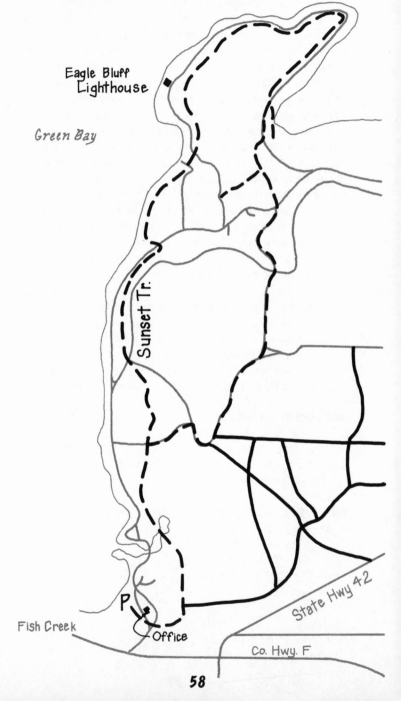

Eagle Bluff
Lighthouse

Green Bay

Sunset Tr.

P

Office

Fish Creek

State Hwy 42

Co. Hwy. F

58

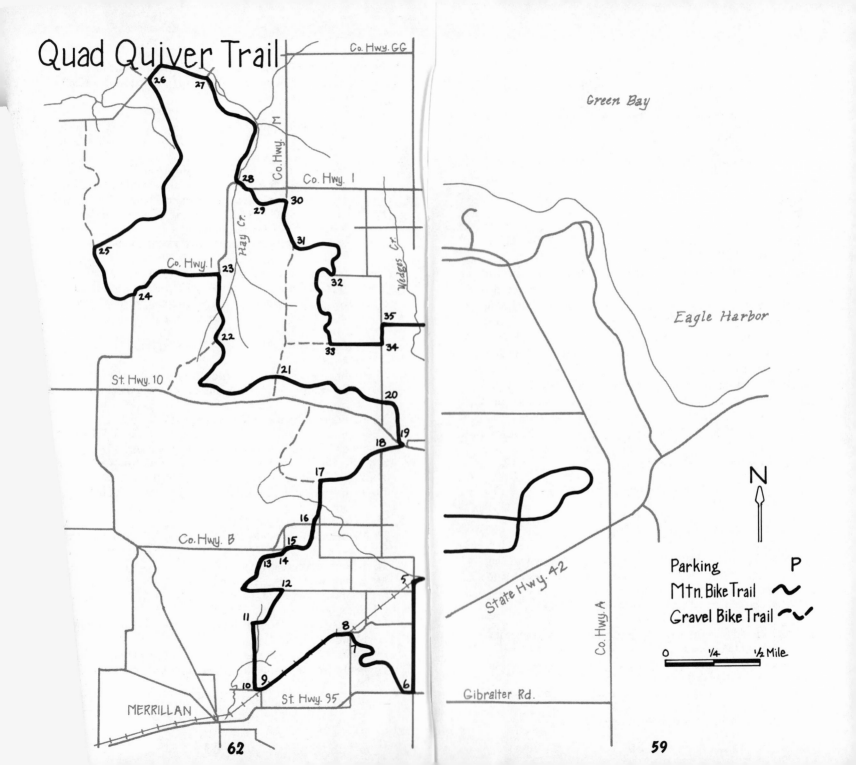

Quad Quiver Trail

Green Bay

Co. Hwy. GG

Eagle Harbor

Co. Hwy. M

Co. Hwy. 1

26 27

28

30

29

31

32

35

33 34

25

Co. Hwy. 1 23

24

22

21

20

19

18

17

St. Hwy. 10

Hay Cr.

Wedges Cr.

16

15

Co. Hwy. B

13 14

12

11

5

8

7

6

10 9

St. Hwy. 95

MERRILLAN

State Hwy. 42

Co. Hwy. A

Gibralter Rd.

N

Parking   P

Mtn. Bike Trail   ～

Gravel Bike Trail   ～

0   1/4   1/2 Mile

Quad Quiver

The ninety-four-mile Quad Quiver, brainchild of Steve Meurett, is the longest one-day organized ATB ride in Wisconsin. The ride makes one long loop through the sand barrens and oak ridges of desolate Clark County Forest and all but three miles are in the dirt. Experienced riders complete this loop in about eight hours—it can take longer if the sand is soft.

We thought we'd include the cue sheet (as written) from the 1995 edition since it's one of the shortest in the ride's history. The more recent versions have been closer to a hundred miles, a century on dirt, a true accomplishment if you can finish this marathon event. If you can't follow directions, you can always join the Neillsville Trail Association for its annual ride in early July. Meurett always promises a good time.

Start on Highway 10 on the western edge of Neillsville and ride west. Bring plenty of food and water because there are precious few stops along the route.

1. Left on River Avenue off Highway 10 (South)
2. Right on Maple Road (West)
3. Left on Columbia Avenue (South)
4. Right on Middle Road (West)
5. Left on Fisher Avenue (South)
6. Right on Highway 95 (West) for one block to Levis parking lot; left on West Levis Loop, left on Trow Trail, and left on Flatlander all the way to Gorman Avenue
7. Right on Gorman Avenue (North) and go about a quarter of a mile
8. Left on old railroad bed (West), don't take ATV trail, which is straight here
9. Right on dirt road, some junk here
10. Right on Kovar Road (North)
11. Right at T intersection (East then Northeast) and stay on Kovar (ATV trail)
12. Left on Poertner Road (West)

13. Right into Wildcat Mound Park; there is a water pump here
14. Right on ATV trail out of park (East) and follow dirt road; it turns left after a quarter of a mile
15. Right on ATV trail across from sand pit (East)
16. cross County Highway B, then take a left (North) at Bruce Mound Avenue (a gravel road and part of ATV trail) which is a half mile or so past County B
17. Right (East) on snowmobile trail (dirt road)
18. take County B a half mile (Northeast) to Wildcat Inn then take ATV trail north out of the parking lot
19. Right on snowmobile trail (North), there are some side trails here but stay on main trail
20. cross Bachelors Avenue (gravel road) keep going west on ATV trail to Wildrock
21. Left on dirt road for fifty yards, turn right (West) onto a logging road/horse trail; there will be blue and red horse signs, pink Buzzard Buster arrows, and lots of grass here
22. Right on dirt road (North), there is a gate here, go right (North) onto Dam 10 Road
23. Left on County I (West), this is three miles of blacktop
24. Right on Koehlers Ford Lane (West then North)
25. Right again, staying on Koehlers Ford Lane (East the North); long haul here
26. Right on gravel road (North then East)
27. Right on Hay Creek Road (South and East); EAT H there is a picnic area and a tavern by the lake
28. cross County I and take a left on ATV trail (sandy
29. Left to Wildrock Lot (Snowmobile Trail 27)
30. Right on Bald Peak Road (South); the Wildrock S is here
31. Left on snowmobile trail (East)
32. Right on Wildwood Road (ATV trail); there is a house here
33. Left on gravel road (East)
34. Left on Bachelors Avenue (North)
35. Right on Chili Road (East)
36. Right on Resewood Avenue (South)
37. Left on South Mound Road (East); cross Co G and keep going East
38. Right on Grand Avenue (South), this is bla
39. follow Grand Avenue into town, turn righ and go up hill to clinic.

St. Hwy 98

Co. Hwy. OO

Black River

Co. Hwy. G

Co. Hwy. H

36

Co. Hwy. G

Co. Hwy. C

37   38

St. Hwy. 10

1   39
P   NEILLSVILLE

3   2

Black River

4

Parking   P
Mtn. Bike Trail ～

N

St. Hwy. 95

0   1   2   3   4 Miles

Numbers Correspond with Text

63

Rib Lake

Every August Ice Age Days comes to the little village of Rib Lake, and the community celebrates the glacial epoch that shaped the surrounding landscape. Landscape that in turn shapes the life of the community. Local nordic skiers developed the Rib Lake Trail System, a trail that in spots runs concurrently with the Ice Age Trail and naturally lends itself to mountain biking.

This is hilly country, like all Ice Age terrain. The annual cross-country ski race held on these trails is called the Hinder Binder because, yes, you can get your hinder in a binder, especially on the downhills.

The western trailhead sits a half mile west of the high school in Rib Lake, on Little Rib Road. The loop used in the Ice Age Classic and the Hinder Binder starts here. The trail gains nearly three hundred vertical feet in the first three kilometers before crossing County Highway D. Between County D and Harper Drive the trail crosses Wiedervereinigkeits Bridge over Sheep Ranch Creek. For those not up on their German, Wiedervereinigkeits means "reunification." The bridge, often very slippery, was dedicated in 1991 on the day East and West Germany were reunited.

The vertical gained in the first few kilometers is typical of the entire trail, so expect little flat riding on this narrow doubletrack. The trail is so narrow in spots—it was originally built for diagonal striding—that the Rib Lake Ski Club has started to widen it to accommodate ski skating—good for skiing, not so good for mountain biking. Besides the climbing, fatigue increases because the surface of Rib Lake Trail always seems spongy. In fact, we checked our tires several times to see if they were flat. You know the feeling. Twenty kilometers over this Ice Age terrain will wear out all but the fittest riders. This trail can also get muddy after rain, so ride responsibly and don't tear up the trail.

The worst section of trail comes between the five and seven kilometer markers, the trail just east of Harper Drive. Clear-cutting and trail widening have wreaked havoc through this section, although time and Mother Nature will heal these wounds. We suggest avoiding at least this section, perhaps the entire trail, after heavy rain. The trail also crosses several trickles and seeps that need to be forded. For those who don't appreciate the wet mud smell of rotting vegetation and reeking methane, this is better done in dry weather.

Past the eleven-kilometer marker, the Ice Age Trail continues east to another trailhead on County Highway C, and the Rib Lake Trail loops back toward the west trailhead. The Timm's Hill National Trail (THNT) spurs off the Ice Age here and winds north. Both the Ice Age and Timm's Hill Trails offer challenging singletrack and plenty of climbing. Eventually, the THNT climbs Timm's Hill, the highest point in the state at 1951.5 feet. Unfortunately, both are out-and-back trails from the eastern trailhead on County C.

Looping back, the Rib Lake Trail runs through Sappy 5 Sugarbush. Look out for the white five-gallon pails during sugar season. At Harper Drive the trail joins the two-way back to the western trailhead, the last three kilometers a downhill ride back to town. Volunteers blazed a mile and a half of singletrack for the 1995 Ice Age Classic. Look for this rough singletrack past Harper Drive.

While in town, check out the burgers and black-and-white photographs of the logging heydays at the Camp 28 Restaurant overlooking the waters of Rib Lake.

Directions: Rib Lake lies east of Highway 13 on Highway 102. The trailhead is west of the high school on Little Rib Road. For information contact the Rib Lake Area Nordic Ski Club, c/o Russ Blennert, W4548 County Highway D, Westboro, Wisconsin 54451. Telephone is 715-427-5830.

Fee: None.

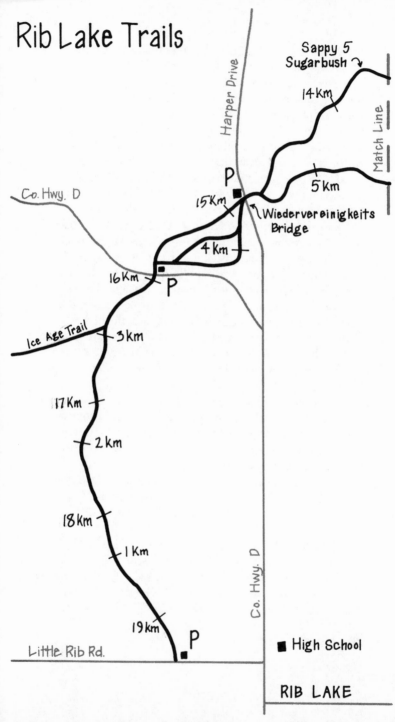

Rib Lake Trails

Sappy 5
Sugarbush

Harper Drive

Match Line

14 km

5 km

P

15 Km

Wiedervereinigkeits
Bridge

Co. Hwy. D

4 km

16 Km

P

Ice Age Trail — 3 km

17 Km

2 km

18 km

1 Km

Co. Hwy. D

19 km

P

Little Rib Rd.

High School

RIB LAKE

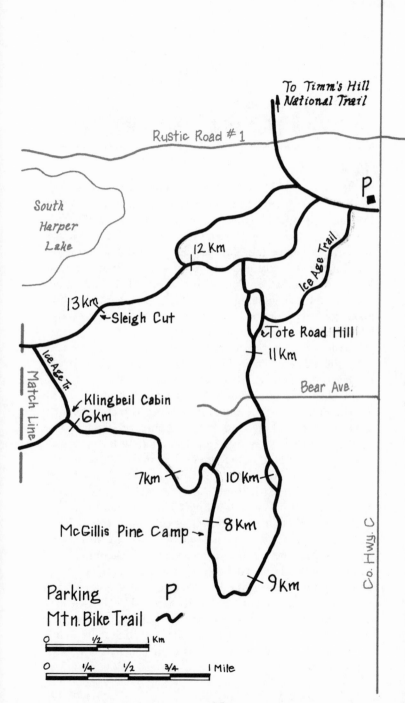

Rib Lake

To Timm's Hill
National Trail

Rustic Road #1

South
Harper
Lake

P

Ice Age Trail

12 Km

13 km
←Sleigh Cut

Tote Road Hill

Ice Age Tr.

11 Km

Bear Ave.

Match Line

Klingbeil Cabin
6 Km

7 km

10 Km

8 Km

McGillis Pine Camp →

9 Km

Co. Hwy. C

Parking   P
Mtn. Bike Trail ～

0   ½   1 Km

0   ¼   ½   ¾   1 Mile

The Underdown

Northeast of Merrill between Highways 51 and 17, the Harrison Hills begin their rising and falling, topping out at Lookout Mountain, at over 1,900 feet, and Irma Hill, the third highest point in Wisconsin. The area's elevation has earned it the name the Northern Highlands. The terrain of this Lincoln County area is typical of that along or near Wisconsin's Ice Age Trail. The undulating hills and numerous small lakes nestled among birch and northern hardwood hills make for excellent mountain bike terrain that few cyclists know about or take advantage of.

Miles of logging roads and cross-country ski trails criss-cross the Underdown Wildlife Area in the southern part of the Harrison Hills. It's somewhat of a maze, and it seems each year a skier, hiker, or mountain biker gets lost in the nearly 7,000 acres. One of the last groups to get lost, cross-country skiers, spent a chilly and fireless February night in the Underdown. Bring a compass and take a look at the maps provided at the trailhead or the USGS Bloomville Quadrangle.

The trails in the Underdown—named after Bill Underdown, an early settler in the area—aren't marked specifically for mountain biking. The ski trail loops are marked well though, as are the equestrian trails. Yes, there are horseback riders in the Underdown. We've yet to meet any on the trails, but have run over evidence of their passing. Expect to see horses and riders only on the weekends, and then probably only the summer holiday weekends. (We've yet to even encounter other mountain bikers here.) The horses have started to blaze singletrack the past few years. However, these gnarly trails are unmarked and haphazard. Ride them only if certain of your orienteering skills or if you have an innate sense of direction.

It's very easy to get lost in the Underdown's maze of trails and logging roads. And local riders have been blazing more and more singletrack each year, which is also unmarked. The ski loops run three distances: the Green Trail is five kilometers, the Red Trail is twelve kilometers, and the Blue Trail is eighteen kilometers. Shortcuts also run between the trails, which in turn cross the Loop Road, so any number of combinations are possible. The Blue Trail takes riders past Mist Lake and through a dense hemlock stand along its shores, one of the most beautiful spots in the Underdown.

Another even longer option is to follow the orange or brown horseshoes of the longest equestrian trail, a nineteen-mile jaunt. Orange goes clockwise, and brown counterclockwise. This trail runs close to the perimeter of the Underdown, up and down some short, steep climbs and through a couple of low swamps. Avoid the mud of these low areas (for those riders who dislike bike cleaning and maintenance) by looking for the singletrack through the brush on higher ground. This outer loop is not that well-marked, so keep alert for the horseshoes—if you don't see one for some time, you're probably lost. If lost, look for the gravel of Loop Road or the better-marked cross-country ski trails, which at times run concurrently with the equestrian trails. If really lost, get out the compass. The Underdown, run jointly by Lincoln County and the DNR, is roughly ten miles northeast of Merrill.

Directions: From Old Highway 51 between Merrill and Tomahawk, take County Highway H east one mile to Copper Lake Road. Then go east on Copper Lake Road a little more than three and a half miles. The parking area is on the right. For information contact the Lincoln County Forestry, Land and Parks Department, Courthouse, Merrill, Wisconsin 54452. Telephone is 800-352-9602.

Fee: Donations are accepted at a drop box at the trailhead.

Underdown Trails

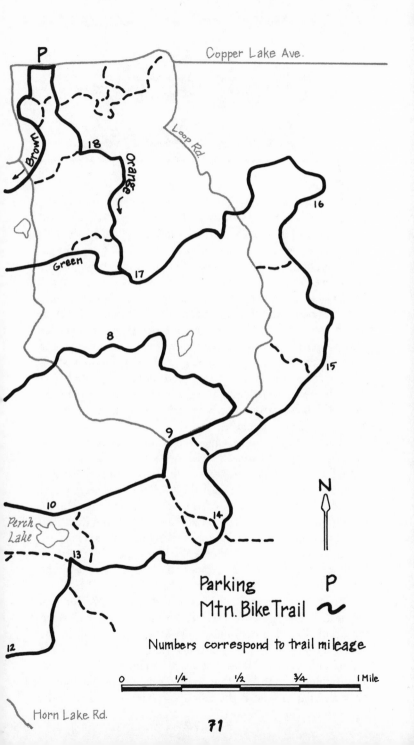

Copper Lake Ave.

P

Brown

Loop Rd.

18

Orange

16

Green

17

8

15

9

N

10

Perch
Lake

14

13

Parking   P

Mtn. Bike Trail

12

Numbers correspond to trail mileage

0   1/4   1/2   3/4   1 Mile

Horn Lake Rd.

Wolf River Territory

Kayakers and trout fishers have long known about the pristine waters of the Wolf River. For decades they have plied the crazy whitewater in search of adventure and fished its deep holes in search of magical trout. Local ATBers hope to add mountain biking to the list of reasons for traveling to the Wolf River area.

In June of 1994, the first three loops totaling thirty miles were mapped, marked, and opened to the public. The Wolf River Territory, founded by local businesses and individuals who support a sustainable economy that will preserve the river and the way of life of the people who depend on it, started the trail system and hopes to add more miles each year. With the help of Nicolet National Forest and the cooperation of the DNR, the group hopes to add more trails and create a network similar to CAMBA.

The existing trails are clustered around the small burg of Langlade, at the crossroads of Highways 64 and 55. Langlade, named after seventeenth-century French explorer Charles Langlade, sits on the banks of the Wolf and has a couple of convenience stores (maps of the trails are at the Mobil), restaurants, and bars. Maps are also available at the Bear Paw Inn. The trail pamphlet suggests parking in Langlade, but we found starting on Van Alstine Road—south and east off Highway 55, just after it crosses the South Branch of the Oconto River—much more convenient.

From here the trail runs both north and south along an abandoned Chicago-Northwestern line and provides access to the South Branch Loop and the Wischer Lake Loop to the north. The 7.7-mile Fish Hatchery Loop starts in Langlade and never leaves the safe confines of pavement and doubletrack. The highlight of the 16.1-mile South Branch Loop, all double-track and flat railway, is the falls about halfway into the ride.

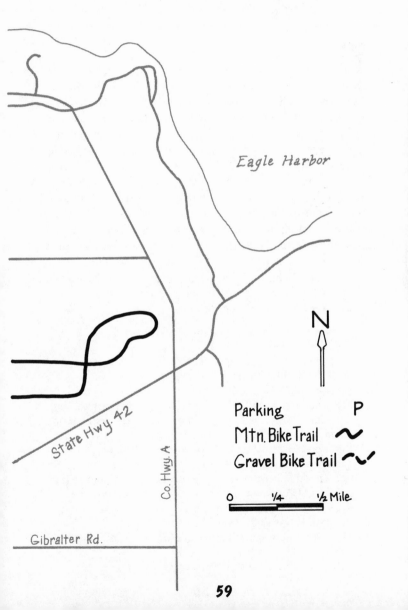

Green Bay

Eagle Harbor

N

Parking   P
Mtn. Bike Trail   ∿
Gravel Bike Trail   ∿

0   ¼   ½ Mile

State Hwy. 42

Co. Hwy. A

Gibralter Rd.

Quad Quiver

The ninety-four-mile Quad Quiver, brainchild of Steve Meurett, is the longest one-day organized ATB ride in Wisconsin. The ride makes one long loop through the sand barrens and oak ridges of desolate Clark County Forest and all but three miles are in the dirt. Experienced riders complete this loop in about eight hours—it can take longer if the sand is soft.

We thought we'd include the cue sheet (as written) from the 1995 edition since it's one of the shortest in the ride's history. The more recent versions have been closer to a hundred miles, a century on dirt, a true accomplishment if you can finish this marathon event. If you can't follow directions, you can always join the Neillsville Trail Association for its annual ride in early July. Meurett always promises a good time.

Start on Highway 10 on the western edge of Neillsville and ride west. Bring plenty of food and water because there are precious few stops along the route.

1. Left on River Avenue off Highway 10 (South)
2. Right on Maple Road (West)
3. Left on Columbia Avenue (South)
4. Right on Middle Road (West)
5. Left on Fisher Avenue (South)
6. Right on Highway 95 (West) for one block to Levis parking lot; left on West Levis Loop, left on Trow Trail, and left on Flatlander all the way to Gorman Avenue
7. Right on Gorman Avenue (North) and go about a quarter of a mile
8. Left on old railroad bed (West), don't take ATV trail, which is straight here
9. Right on dirt road, some junk here
10. Right on Kovar Road (North)
11. Right at T intersection (East then Northeast) and stay on Kovar (ATV trail)
12. Left on Poertner Road (West)

Rib Lake

Every August Ice Age Days comes to the little village of Rib Lake, and the community celebrates the glacial epoch that shaped the surrounding landscape. Landscape that in turn shapes the life of the community. Local nordic skiers developed the Rib Lake Trail System, a trail that in spots runs concurrently with the Ice Age Trail and naturally lends itself to mountain biking.

This is hilly country, like all Ice Age terrain. The annual cross-country ski race held on these trails is called the Hinder Binder because, yes, you can get your hinder in a binder, especially on the downhills.

The western trailhead sits a half mile west of the high school in Rib Lake, on Little Rib Road. The loop used in the Ice Age Classic and the Hinder Binder starts here. The trail gains nearly three hundred vertical feet in the first three kilometers before crossing County Highway D. Between County D and Harper Drive the trail crosses Wiedervereinigkeits Bridge over Sheep Ranch Creek. For those not up on their German, Wiedervereinigkeits means "reunification." The bridge, often very slippery, was dedicated in 1991 on the day East and West Germany were reunited.

The vertical gained in the first few kilometers is typical of the entire trail, so expect little flat riding on this narrow doubletrack. The trail is so narrow in spots—it was originally built for diagonal striding—that the Rib Lake Ski Club has started to widen it to accommodate ski skating—good for skiing, not so good for mountain biking. Besides the climbing, fatigue increases because the surface of Rib Lake Trail always seems spongy. In fact, we checked our tires several times to see if they were flat. You know the feeling. Twenty kilometers over this Ice Age terrain will wear out all but the

St. Hwy 98

Co. Hwy. 00

Black River

Co. Hwy. G

Co. Hwy. H

Co. Hwy. G

Co. Hwy. C

36

37

38

St. Hwy.10

1

39

NEILLSVILLE

3

2

P

4

Black River

Parking   P

Mtn. Bike Trail ∼

N

St. Hwy. 95

0   1   2   3   4 Miles

Numbers Correspond with Text
63

13. Right into Wildcat Mound Park; there is a water pump here
14. Right on ATV trail out of park (East) and follow dirt road; it turns left after a quarter of a mile
15. Right on ATV trail across from sand pit (East)
16. cross County Highway B, then take a left (North) at Bruce Mound Avenue (a gravel road and part of ATV trail) which is a half mile or so past County B
17. Right (East) on snowmobile trail (dirt road)
18. take County B a half mile (Northeast) to Wildcat Inn then take ATV trail north out of the parking lot
19. Right on snowmobile trail (North), there are some side trails here but stay on main trail
20. cross Bachelors Avenue (gravel road) keep going west on ATV trail to Wildrock
21. Left on dirt road for fifty yards, turn right (West) onto a logging road/horse trail; there will be blue and red horse signs, pink Buzzard Buster arrows, and lots of grass here
22. Right on dirt road (North), there is a gate here, go right (North) onto Dam 10 Road
23. Left on County I (West), this is three miles of blacktop
24. Right on Koehlers Ford Lane (West then North)
25. Right again, staying on Koehlers Ford Lane (East then North); long haul here
26. Right on gravel road (North then East)
27. Right on Hay Creek Road (South and East); EAT HERE, there is a picnic area and a tavern by the lake
28. cross County I and take a left on ATV trail (sandy trail here)
29. Left to Wildrock Lot (Snowmobile Trail 27)
30. Right on Bald Peak Road (South); the Wildrock Shelter is here
31. Left on snowmobile trail (East)
32. Right on Wildwood Road (ATV trail); there is an old farm house here
33. Left on gravel road (East)
34. Left on Bachelors Avenue (North)
35. Right on Chili Road (East)
36. Right on Resewood Avenue (South)
37. Left on South Mound Road (East); cross County Highway G and keep going East
38. Right on Grand Avenue (South), this is blacktop
39. follow Grand Avenue into town, turn right at IGA, and go up hill to clinic.

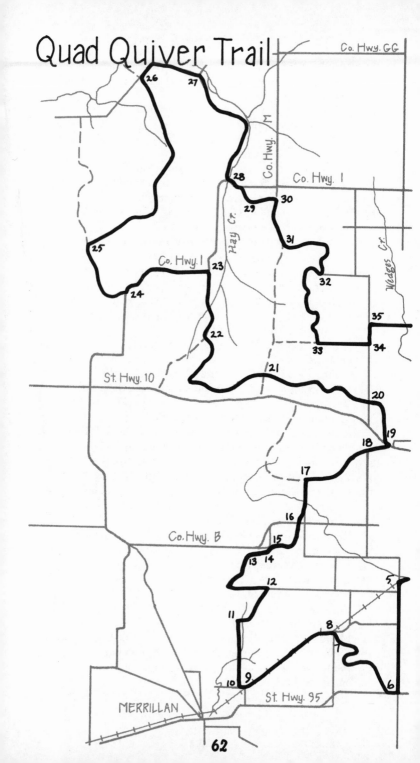

The bank next to this surging rapids, which drop five or six feet, also makes an excellent picnic or camping spot. Look for the Give a Hoot Don't Pollute sculpture here as well. A person could do worse than riding in with a pack, setting up camp for a night or two, and exploring the country surrounding the South Branch of the Oconto. The quickest way to the rapids is to turn left when the trail diverges two miles into the ride. Veering right at this Y junction takes the long loop back around to the rapids. Look closely for the blue signs. Loggers had knocked down at least two signs and momentarily confused us.

The 12.5-mile Wischer Lake Loop is the most difficult of the three. Its difficulty stems from the rock-strewn climbs, not from technical singletrack. This loop starts north on the abandoned railway where it crosses Van Alstine, goes right, or east, of Highway 64 for a half mile, and enters the Nicolet National Forest on Forest Road 2118. The trail goes from pavement to gravel to doubletrack to rutted logging road. In other words, this loop gets progressively more difficult. Just past Perch Lake, a small lake huddled down in a bowl, the stony logging road makes an abrupt granny-gear ascent, an ascent with a view of the surrounding area. This loop finishes up on Forest Service Roads 2336 and 2283, where the ditches and adjacent woodlands were carpeted with trillions of trilliums the late-May afternoon that we rode, before it returns to the pavement of Highway 64.

The Wolf River trails make for excellent family riding. The trails, with their rolling hills, offer more challenge than the typical state trail. Camping, kayaking, and fishing are added reasons to visit. For those ATBers wanting expert-level trails or big woods, choose another trail system. Perhaps in a few years the Wolf River Territory will accommodate those desires.

Directions: The trailhead sits at the intersection of Highways 64 and 55. Staff at the Bear Paw Inn can also provide directions. They're located two miles south of Langlade on the west side of Highway 55.

Fee: None.

Wolf River Territory Trails

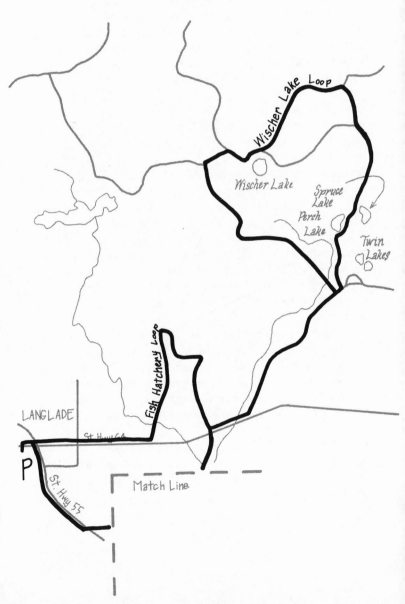

Wischer Lake Loop

Wischer Lake

Spruce
Lake
Perch
Lake

Twin
Lakes

Fish Hatchery Loop

LANGLADE

St. Hwy 64

P

St. Hwy 55

Match Line

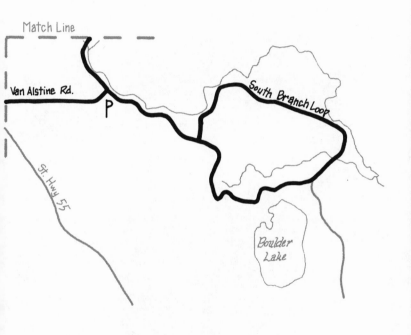

Match Line

Van Alstine Rd.

South Branch Loop

P

St. Hwy 55

Boulder
Lake

Parking   P
Mtn. Bike Trail ∿

N

0   1   2   3 Miles

Rib Lake ★ ★ Underdown ★ Wolf River

★ Nine Mile

Quad Quiver ★

Newport
Peninsula

The
Central
Shorts

Baird Creek

Baird Creek flows through the city of Green Bay and eventually into the bay itself, creating a drainage through the east side of the city. For mountain bikers, this drainage means vertical terrain and technical riding, all within minutes of more than 100,000 people.

All totaled, we'd estimate there are about fifteen miles of trail here, which would take an experienced rider a couple of hours to cover. This isn't a place for first-time riders, and the names of some of the landmarks should warn of what to expect: Superman Hill, Clavicle Hill, the Black Hole, and the Gravity Cavity. Expect sharp drops and climbs, exposed roots, downed logs, and water crossings.

This is a place for experienced riders to sharpen their skills. Rumor has it that 1998 and 1999 WORS Expert Champion Rick Blaser got his start here, riding a BMX bike. We've ridden behind him through singletrack and know that Baird has been a fine school.

Directions: From I-43 North take the Mason Street Exit right or east, then the next left, which is Superior. Superior, a frontage road along the interstate, crosses under the highway and eventually leads to the parking lots at Baird. For more detailed directions stop at In Competition close-by at 2439 University Avenue. The phone number there is 920-465-1510.

Bear Paw Inn

The Bear Paw Inn is a delightful place to visit in any season. The staff here offers activities year-round for cross-country and telemark skiers, snowshoers, kayakers, whitewater canoeists, hikers, campers, and flyfishers. With the development of new singletrack, add mountain bikers to that list.

Currently, the Bear Paw Inn has about ten miles of doubletrack ski trail and a smaller percentage of new singletrack. Soon, though, with the addition of more and more miles of singletrack, the Bear Paw Inn hopes to have about fifteen miles of mountain bikeable trail on their property, adjacent private property, and public land along the Wolf River. It's also a short ride east from their trails to the Wolf River Territory trails in the nearby Nicolet National Forest.

Mountain bikers can ride the existing ski trails, which climb some short, steep, rocky hills, or the recently blazed and much more technical singletrack. This singletrack, marked by orange surveyor's tape, winds around rocks, maple, birch, white pine, and hemlock. It's true singletrack and a delight to ride, especially the Dewberry Trail where it skirts the whitewater of the Wolf.

Billing itself as a bed and breakfast/outdoor recreation center, mountain bikers can overnight at the Bear Paw Inn in a tent, a rustic cabin, or the more luxurious main building. Besides bikes, the center also rents canoes and kayaks, and offers many different classes and workshops too numerous to mention.

Directions: The compound is located two miles south of Langlade on the west side of Highway 55. For information contact Bear Paw Inn, N3494 Highway 55, White Lake, Wisconsin 54491. Telephone is 715-882-3502, email is bearpaw@newnorth.net, and website is www.bearpawinn.com.

Berkhahn Rookery Bicycle Loop

There probably isn't any easier loop in this book than the Berkhahn Trail in the Mead Wildlife Area. Its 6.6 miles (approximately ten kilometers) quietly flow along dikes through marshy lowlands known mostly to waterfowl hunters. Expect no technical challenges, no climbing, single-track, or even sharp corners.

On the other hand, there's hardly a better place in the state to go birding, which is why the Aldo Leopold Chapter of the Audubon Society spent three years lobbying for and developing this trail. First of all, the trail circles the Berkhahn Flowage, home to one of the largest heron rookeries in the state. The rookery grew so large that dozens of great blue herons have since colonized other areas, most notably a spit of land in Lake Wausau.

Besides the herons, many other species inhabit the 28,000 acres of the Mead. Mallards, bluewing teal, and wood ducks are numerous. Around sunset they fly in from feeding areas, their wings whistling overhead. Canada geese, grebes, cormorants, woodcock, and several types of songbirds also make their homes in the Mead. We've even heard rumors of a trumpeter swan in residence. Bring binoculars and your Peterson guide.

To avoid conflicts with hunters, whose fees helped establish the Mead, the trail is open from May 15 to September 1. The trail opens late to minimize human contact with the wildlife during their crucial nesting period, and it closes early to keep bicyclists from inadvertently flushing waterfowl. Hopefully with this compromise, everybody is reasonably happy.

Directions: The trailhead and Mead Wildlife Area head-quarters are on County Highway S. Take I-39 to Highway 34. Go west three miles to County C, continue west on C about twelve miles, and turn left, or south, on County S.

Big Eau Pleine County Park

Big Eau Pleine County Park occupies a narrow peninsula jutting two miles into the Big Eau Pleine Reservoir. A total of 9.4 miles of doubletrack, groomed for classic skiing in winter, traces the perimeter of the peninsula including many of its tiny bays. The water is always in view while riding here. The trails, mostly flat and not technical, travel through mature, mostly sugar maple, woods. The east section of the trail runs through some low, soggy areas, while the western section gains a bit of altitude and tends to be drier. With nearly a hundred camping sites, Eau Pleine gets busy on summer weekends. Watch for deer—the population stays high because there's no hunting allowed inside the park.

Directions: From Mosinee take Highway 153 west six miles to Eau Pleine Park Road, then south on Eau Pleine Park Road to the park. Telephone is 715-847-5235.

Brown County Reforestation Camp

Eight miles of cross-country ski trails, open to mountain bikes, wind through this county forest, compliments of the Bay Shore Bicycle Club's lobbying efforts. Most of the trails are doubletrack, some grassy and some sandy. The Reforestation Camp—so-named because the tax-delinquent property was reforested by inmates of the Brown County Jail—offers off-road riding close to the large urban area in the Fox Valley.

Although much of the terrain at the Reforestation Camp is flat, the Camp hosts an annual WORS race. The most interesting trails, the ski trails Maples and Birches, have a slight roll. There is room for singletrack development if the county or local riders would take some initiative. After riding, visit the zoo in the middle of the camp. In fact, with the zoo and the moderate trails, the Reforestation Camp is one of the more ideal places in Wisconsin for a family outing.

Directions: Take Highways 41/141 north from Green Bay, exit onto County Highway B at Suamico, and take this two miles west to County IR. Go north on IR about eight tenths of a mile to the parking lot on the right, next to the observation tower. More parking is available over the hill across from the zoo.

Crocker Hills

The Crocker Hills lie in a 15,000-acre triangle bounded by Highways 52, 55, and 64 in eastern Langlade County. Although this isn't a true wilderness area since it's been heavily logged and ATVers routinely buzz up and down the double-track roads, this chunk of land sprawls over a township-sized area. Which means there's plenty of country to get turned around and lost in here. These hills, owned mostly by Nekoosa Papers and Langlade County, are the highest in the county, offering mountain bikers rugged and extensive terrain.

The Crocker Hills have untapped mountain bike potential, but few riders know about or ride here yet. Hunters, ATVers, snowmobilers, and mushers use this land extensively, their trails crisscrossing the undulating hills. In winter mushers run their dog teams through the Crocker Hills and have even marked (with blue signs) some of their loops, especially in the southern end. Most of the riding here is either rough gravel or double-track logging roads—all of it unmarked for cyclists.

In other words, this isn't the place for novice riders or inexperienced navigators. The loops are long and difficult, and it's one of the few places listed in this book where a GPS might come in handy. For those who would like to explore the Crocker Hills, get a USGS map and compass and bring along plenty of food and water. All the difficulties do have their reward—the Crocker Hills is the only place where Mark has seen two Cooper's Hawks in one day.

Directions: Mountain bikers can get into the hills from many access points. One of the best is Smokey Road, which intersects Highway 64 on the eastern edge of Elton. Take this road north until you find a suitable place to park on the gravel. Then ride. For more information contact the Bear Paw Inn, N3494 Highway 55, White Lake, Wisconsin 54491. Telephone is 715-882-3502, email is bearpaw@newnorth.net, and website is www.bearpawinn.com.

The Green Circle

The Green Circle—a twenty-four-mile loop around Stevens Point—is perhaps the most unusual trail in this book. Unusual because at times it resembles a state trail on an abandoned rail corridor, while at other times it rides like a true mountain bike trail. It's also unusual because of how it came to be.

The Green Circle is the best example in the state of community members pooling together resources and creating a useful and valuable trail. This meandering, crushed-granite trail travels through private, university, city, and county land, bringing together private landowners, the University of Wisconsin–Stevens Point (UWSP), public utilities, local government, state and federal agencies, and most importantly, individual community members. If only we could have more trails like this circling our communities in our state.

Mountain bikers can get on the Green Circle in hundreds of different spots. A good jumping-off point for out-of-town-ers would be the Hilltop Bar on Highway 10, just west of I-39. Two blocks west of the bar, take Ridge Road north and the trail begins and shortly enters the woods. We started from a friend's apartment and rode a couple blocks to where the trail intersected Patch Street and McDill Pond, a flowage on the Plover River. From here we rode north, jumping into the woods along the west bank of the Plover, which the trail follows on the river's eastern edge.

After skirting the Stevens Point Airport, often through red pine plantations, the trail drops down into the Schmeeckle Reserve, a UWSP field campus, and circles Lake Joanis. The Green Circle Trail continues west until it runs into its western border at the Wisconsin River. It follows the river's eastern bank south through the downtown area, passing a few blocks from the historic Stevens Point Brewery, which gives daily tours. South of downtown, the trail treks through land owned by Stora Enso, and it's here along the river bottomland that we spotted two unconcerned bucks, both still in velvet since it was late June. Locals say the mosquitoes can be bad along here at times, but we had no bug troubles.

Moving east, the Green Circle travels away from the Wisconsin River and back toward the Plover. The trail eventually turns north and runs through a residential area, sometimes right through backyards. Here we met several joggers, hikers, and some dog walkers. This is a multiple use trail, and trail organizers suggest that cyclists limit their speed to ten miles per hour. They also suggest walking bikes over the many wooden bridges that span low lying, muddy areas. These bridges, some off-camber, do get slippery when wet.

Although the Green Trail won't challenge an expert rider's technical skills, it does offer nearly twenty-four miles of clearly marked riding, plus the amenities of an urban area. More cities need trails like this.

For information contact the Stevens Point Area Foundation–Green Circle, 2442 Sims Avenue, Stevens Point, Wisconsin 54481.

Harrison Hills Segment of the Ice Age Trail

The Ice Age Trail snakes its way through Lincoln County, through some rough country, through some big country. One of the most technical singletrack rides in Wisconsin starts in the Turtle Lake region and eventually crawls up 1,900-foot Lookout Mountain. In summer the ferns grow high and clog chainring and cogs, and the mosquitoes and black flies can be merciless. Nevertheless, the ride and the view from the tower end all misgivings about the conditions, which in spring and fall are much more forgiving, more tolerable, more enjoyable.

Getting up to Lookout Mountain isn't easy. At times, it's difficult to follow the yellow blaze marks on the Ice Age Trail, especially where logging has changed the area recently. Blowdowns and the work of industrious beavers force numerous dismounts. Some of the climbs also require pushing, especially the last effort up the mountain. The end does justify the means, though. From the tower (staffed by the DNR, especially in spring before green-up) the surrounding country unfolds: Rib Mountain to the south; Irma Hill, the third highest point in the state, and the fire tower at Rock Falls to the southeast; and directly east, the broad valley of the Prairie River, one of Wisconsin's finest trout fisheries. On a clear day, the view stretches north to the lookout on Squirrel Hill, southwest of Minocqua. Check around the tower lookout for raspberries in season.

The Ice Age Trail continues from the fire tower north to County Highway B and again north by northeast, where it crosses Highway 17. The trail from County B to Highway 17 meanders past several small lakes and an old abandoned ski area. All are ridable sections. However, the section from Turtle Lake Road to the tower is the most scenic as well as most difficult. The total distance from Turtle Lake Road to Highway 17 is about twelve and a quarter miles.

Directions: From Highway 51 take County Highway J east 5.8 miles, then Turtle Lake Road north. A half mile down Turtle Lake park in the ATV lot on the west side of the road. The Ice Age intersects Turtle Lake a mile farther north. We suggest familiarizing yourself with the *Wisconsin Atlas and Gazetteer* or USGS maps before venturing here. It is big country and easy to get lost in.

Jack Lake County Park

This Langlade County park and forest is home to slightly more than fourteen miles of cross-country ski trails that have recently doubled as mountain bike trails in the off-season. These doubletrack trails range up and down glaciated hills typical of the Ice Age Trail, which runs through the area then off to the northwest. Maple, birch, hemlock, and spruce line the trails.

Jack Lake makes for a good family weekend outing—the trails aren't technical, so the kids shouldn't have problems plus there's primitive camping available along the lake. So bring the tent, the Coleman burner, and definitely the bikes.

Directions: Take Highway 45 twelve miles north of Antigo. Turn right, or east, and go two miles on County Highway J and turn right at Park Road which runs into Veterans Memorial Park. For information contact the Antigo Chamber of Commerce, 329 Superior Street, Antigo, Wisconsin 54409. Telephone is 715-623-4134. Langlade County Forester telephone is 715-627-6236.

Lake Wissota State Park

These, too, are easy, family-style trails along the banks of Lake Wissota, a dammed section of the Chippewa River. The ski and horseback trails, which are all open to mountain bikes, total ten miles. Some of the hiking trails are closed to mountain bikes. Camping spots abound. Jacob Leinenkugel's Brewery—a must see—is located on the north side of nearby Chippewa Falls and conducts tours weekdays and Saturday.

Directions: Eight miles northeast of Chippewa Falls on County Highway S. For information contact Lake Wissota State Park, RR 8, Box 360, Chippewa Falls, Wisconsin 54729. Telephone is 715-382-4574.

Medford District of the Chequamegon National Forest

Known as the other Chequamegon, the little brother of the more often visited northern districts, this little known region remains untapped for mountain biking, even though it has immense potential. At the Perkinstown Winter Sports Area, a mile south of Perkinstown, the Forest Service has mapped twenty kilometers of trails that are used mainly by cross-country skiers. These also double as mountain bike trails when the snow isn't around.

Besides these trails, hundreds of miles of gravel roads, logging roads, doubletrack, ATV, and hunter walking trails lie within the national forest boundaries. A section of the Ice Age Trail also meanders through here. Camp here at several National Forest Campgrounds—we suggest Mondeaux Dam. We strongly suggest bringing a compass and riding with the Forest Service map. Get a USGS map of this ranger district of the national forest at the USDA Forest Service headquarters on Highway 13 in Medford. Then ride.

Directions: From Highway 13 five miles north of Medford, take County Highway M fifteen miles west to Perkinstown, which is the best place to start riding. For information contact the USDA Forest Service, 1170 S. Fourth Avenue, Park Falls, Wisconsin 54552. Telephone is 715-762-2461.

New Wood Wildlife Area

Flat to rolling doubletrack winds through second, third, and fourth growth woods here. The Ice Age Trail meanders west to east through New Wood, mostly along the New Wood River, and it's open to riding here. A state wildlife area, New Wood is known for its wolf pack. This is a remote area, even though it's not all that far north in the state. Thousands of acres and relatively few roads crossing the area make it ideal wolf habitat. It's also excellent mountain biking habitat. Many low swampy spots punctuate New Wood, one reason for the lack of improved roads. However, most of the swamps can be circumnavigated easily.

This area receives heavy hunting pressure, particularly during gun deer season, although it is also excellent grouse-ward. Stay away during gun deer season, unless you're using a mountain bike to hunt deer (not a bad idea). Usually by gun deer season, however, New Wood is snow-covered and difficult to ride.

Directions: From Merrill take Highway 107 west to County Highway E. Head north on E for thirteen miles, then west on Conservation Avenue a long mile. Look for walking trails to the north and south off Conservation.

Otter Lake

This area lies roughly ten miles north of the Underdown in the Lincoln County Forest. There are no official mountain bike loops here, just miles and miles of logging roads, ATV trails, and the Otter Lake Ski Trails. One of our favorite rides is on some of the doubletrack in the area. From Otter Lake, where camping is available, take the park road back to Bear Trail Road. Turn left, or east, on Bear Trail and take that all the way to Turtle Lake Road. A bit of Bear Trail, maybe half a mile, is paved. Turn right, or south, on Turtle Lake into the heart of the Harrison Hills. Turtle Lake runs south/southwest and eventually hits the pavement of County Highway J, and from there it's about five miles to the Underdown. For a mammoth ride, thirty to fifty miles, start at Otter Lake, ride to and around the Underdown, then back to Otter Lake. Chequamegon Fat Tire 40 training, for sure.

For a shorter ride, take a right, or west, off Turtle Lake onto Beaver Trail, which is poorly marked. This trail is near the brown Ice Age Trail markers. Beaver Trail runs into Cranefoot Lake Road, which runs into Grundy Road, a long, flat, granite stretch straight north and back to Bear Trail and Otter Lake. Many ATV trails intersect Turtle Lake and Bear Trail, one running up to Lookout Mountain. You can also make a long gradual climb to the summit of Lookout Mountain by taking the service road off County Highway B, just past B's intersection with Highway 17.

Otter Lake Campground offers a dozen sites on the north shore of the lake. Camping is allowed in most places in the Lincoln County Forest. The USGS Parrish and Harrison maps show all the lakes, hills, and roads in the area.

Directions: From Highway 51, sixteen miles north of Merrill, go east on County Highway S to its intersection with County Highway H. County S ends, but continue east on Stevenson Road to Grundy Road. Go left, or north, on Grundy a few hundred yards to Bear Trail Road. Follow the Otter Lake Campground signs from there.

Tigerton

The Tigerton Lumber Company holds extensive tracts of land throughout this area of the state. Since the company manages some of its holdings for timber, not pulp, the trees tend to be larger than those on paper company land. In the past few years, the logging company has begun promoting some of its land's recreational value as a public relations venture. The company has mapped and marked ten miles of trail, mostly logging roads, in 6,700 acres near its home office. The trails run up and down some moderate-sized hills and through some interesting terrain.

Directions: Maps are available in downtown Tigerton, home of the infamous Posse Comitatus, or by writing Tigerton Main Street Inc., P.O. Box 3, Tigerton, Wisconsin 54486. Telephone is 715-535-2110. Or contact the Tigerton Area Council of Tourism, P.O. Box 307, Tigerton, Wisconsin 54486-0307.

Perrot

Nepco Lake
Trail

Calumet

High Cliff

Bluebird Springs

Mirror Lake

Devil's Head

Kickapoo Valley
Reserve

Devil's Lake

Yellow River

Quarry
Park

Blue Mound

Cam-Rock

Area 25.5

Badger
Prairie

Lapham Peak

The Southern Trails

Black River State Forest

The Black River State Forest lies in a land of solitary bluffs, buttes, and mounds. It is a land that unexpectedly resembles the plateau country out west in Utah or Wyoming, not the pastoral landscape that typically comes to mind when imagining the Dairy State. Here, castle-like buttes and tepee-like mounds rise out of an unusually flat and broad plain. The long views from atop these mounds reinforce the Big Sky feel of this place east of the Mississippi in west central Wisconsin. Scrubby jack pine and red oak cover both mound and plain, growing up out of white, sandy, arid soil. Cacti grow in the sandy breaks between the trees. Yes, cacti in Wisconsin.

Like the West, this stark terrain makes for good mountain biking. Black River's sandy trail system is divided into two parts—Smrekar and Wildcat. Parking for Wildcat is located almost smack-dab in the middle of both trail systems on North Settlement Road, making it a good place to park. On peak weekends this lot may get crowded, but more parking is available in the Smrekar lot, a mile north of County Highway O on Smrekar Road.

The Norway Pine, Red Oak, and Wildcat Trails offer the most aerobic and technical challenge of the trails at Black River. The Wildcat loop dishes out some tough granny-gear climbs—some chain-snapping stuff—including the long grind up Wildcat Mound. Smrekar's terrain is somewhat flatter than Wildcat, but half again as long, roughly eight miles. So pick your poison—short and hilly or long and flat. The trails, originally doubletrack designed for cross-country skiing, pose little technical difficulty other than deep, front-wheel-grabbing sand on some descents. Or the sandy soil may break loose on the steeper climbs, forcing a dismount and some pushing. Most riders, all but the most inexperienced, should have few surprises at Black River. A constant barrage of climbs does, however, make Black River difficult physically. Up, down, up, down, the trail never seems to flatten as it winds around the bluffs and mounds.

But the many climbs are worth every wheezing gasp and pounding heartbeat, every skipping chain and loss of traction. They are worth it because of the views, panoramas that seem pristine even today. The DNR has built wooden benches on the lips of many of the scenic overlooks, and it's seductively easy to fall into a rhythm of laboring up the climbs and recovering on the benches. Finding an excuse to rest isn't difficult.

Some singletrack, less than a mile total, detours off the main trail to reach a couple of the scenic overlooks. The detour about a mile from the climb up Wildcat Mound is moderately difficult, an invitation for those who like singletrack. We've heard rumblings about more singletrack being built here, yet as we go to press no new trail has been blazed. With more singletrack the Black River State Forest would rival Levis Mound.

Camping is allowed in most places in the state forests, although a camping permit is required. Shale Road runs close by Wildcat Mound, making it one of the easiest mounds to get gear to and camp on. Those who prefer a rougher experience can pedal deeper into the woods, away from the noise of any internal combustion engines happening by or any loopy mountain bikers howling at the moon from the top of a mound.

Directions: From its intersection with I-94 take County Highway O east four miles to North Settlement Road. Then go north one mile to the parking lot on the left. For information contact the Black River State Forest, 910 Highway 54 East, Black River Falls, Wisconsin 54615. Telephone is 715-284-1440.

Fee: A Wisconsin Parks vehicle sticker and a trail pass are required.

Black River State Forest Trails

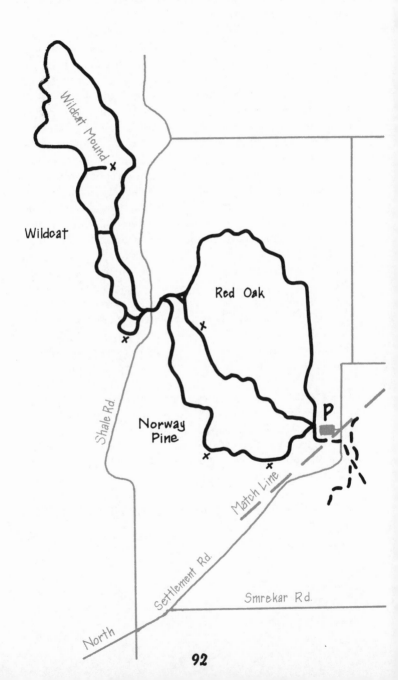

Wildcat Mound

Wildcat

Red Oak

Shale Rd.

Norway
Pine

P

Match Line

Settlement Rd.

North

Smrekar Rd.

Yonkers Rd.

North

Match Line

North

Smrekar Rd

Ridge

Central

P

Parking   P
Mtn. Bike Trail   ~
Overlook   x

South

Co. Hwy O

0   1/4   1/2   3/4   1 Mile

N

Governor Dodge State Park

Governor Dodge didn't exactly thrill us from the start. We climbed out of Cox Hollow from the parking lot at the concession area, up the ridge on the combination hiking/mountain bike/cross-country ski trail. It is pavement all the way to the top—nice, smooth pavement, the kind found on golf cart paths. This is good for golf, bad for mountain biking. We learned later that the DNR paved this section because it joins the park with the Military Ridge Trail, an abandoned railway since converted to a bike and snowmobile trail that runs to the south of the park. We turned left at the top of the ridge onto Mill Creek Trail, a 3.3-mile segment of dirt and grass, and we continued on, faith restored.

Halfway through Mill Creek Trail, at the rest stop among walnut trees, we stopped and took in the view of the limestone formations lying below on the north shore of Twin Valley Lake. Mill Creek, a wide ski trail, meanders through overgrown field and pasture once farmed in better times when the prairie soil was still fertile. Much of the 5,000-plus acres at Governor Dodge was once farmed by homesteaders taking advantage of the rich black prairie soil that capped the ridges of this part of the Driftless Area in southwestern Wisconsin.

Past the rest area a sign shouts: STEEP DOWNGRADE AND CURVES AHEAD. The DNR posted this sign for good reason. The trail quickly loses the elevation gained coming up the pavement, all in a rush, and it's back to the parking lot. Be careful on the descent.

Meadow Valley Trail, a 6.8-mile segment, begins, like Mill Creek, at the parking lot by Cox Hollow Lake. This trail also starts by climbing up out of the valley to the ridge tops and views of the surrounding Frank Lloyd Wright country. It's a bit confusing trying to follow the DNR's signs around the park as horse, hiking, and cycling trails combine and cross. But like most state parks, it's tough to get lost on the mountain biking trails, they're that well-marked.

Also like Mill Creek, the wide Meadow Valley Trail meanders through field and pasture. The trail makes one early foray into the woods, past an old limestone foundation surrounded by large white pine. The white pine look strangely Northwoodsy in a land of oak, basswood, and shagbark hickory.

The second half gets more interesting. The trail descends back to the valley and the lake. Once again there are no surprises since the DNR has posted all the tricky descents. Surprises mean excitement but also potential lawsuits. The final short descent is covered by baseball-size limestone, stuff difficult to navigate and not fun to fall on. Take it easy here.

The ten miles of trail at Governor Dodge are neither technically nor aerobically taxing, although if ridden hard the climbs can definitely burn. Those seeking singletrack nirvana should go elsewhere. Unfortunately, the equestrians have double the trail mileage of the cyclists, even though the two wheelers outnumber the four leggers. Perhaps in the future the DNR will open more trails to riding or blaze some singletrack. The surrounding country is beautiful, and the park is close to the masses in the southern part of the state clamoring for more trail.

Directions: Governor Dodge is located three miles north of Dodgeville off Highway 23. For information contact Governor Dodge State Park, 4175 State Road, Dodgeville, Wisconsin 53533. Telephone is 608-935-2315.

Fee: A Wisconsin Parks vehicle sticker and a trail pass are required.

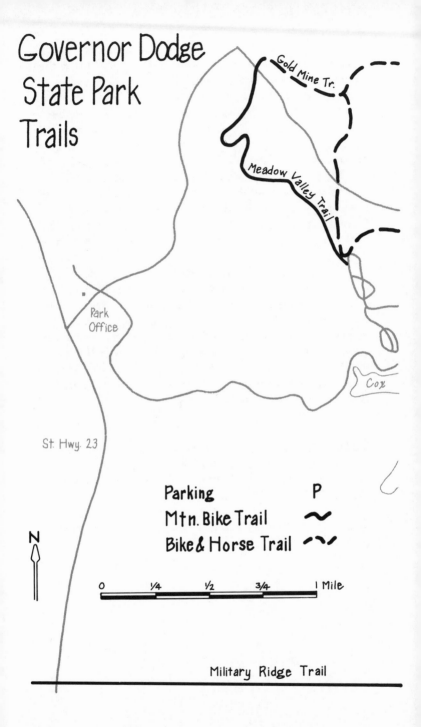

Governor Dodge
State Park
Trails

Gold Mine Tr.

Meadow Valley Trail

Park
Office

Cox

St. Hwy. 23

Parking   P
Mtn. Bike Trail   ~
Bike & Horse Trail ~

N

0   ¼   ½   ¾   1 Mile

Military Ridge Trail

96

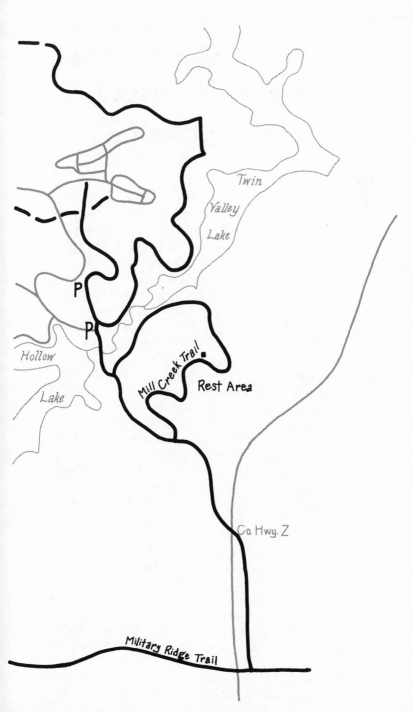

Twin
Valley
Lake

P
P

Hollow
Lake

Mill Creek Trail

Rest Area

Co Hwy. Z

Military Ridge Trail

Kettle Moraine State Forest
Northern Unit

The Northern Unit of the Kettle Moraine State Forest looks every bit like its renowned cousin, the Southern Kettles. The same glacial forces that molded and carved some of Wisconsin's most celebrated terrain shaped both state forests. The ridges and kettles present the same characteristic sharpness and intimacy, while the flora and fauna appear identical.

Likewise, the mountain biking is similar: same terrain, same trail surface, same scenery. Both have also had controversy. The Southern Kettles has faced overcrowding and erosion problems, while the Northern Kettles has faced opposition from local cross-country skiers fearing erosion problems. Fortunately, all groups concerned are working together to solve trail conflicts.

The lack of crowds at the Northern Kettles is a noticeable and welcome difference. We met only two other riders on a July weekday. Unlike our experience at the Southern Kettles we didn't have difficulty finding a parking spot and we didn't have to dodge other riders. We didn't have to negotiate slippery plastic mats like those put down by the DNR at the Southern Kettles to control the erosion caused by thousands of soil-churning knobbies. We didn't have to deal with a park ranger packing a 9 mm Glock. All things considered, we enjoyed our experience at the Northern Kettles much more.

Like the Southern Kettles, the Northern Unit has two trail systems: Greenbush and New Fane. The Greenbush Trails are more challenging and scenic than New Fane's, and its ten miles easily doubles the mileage at New Fane, which the DNR lists as seven, but is more like four because the trails run contiguously at times. Unlike the Southern Kettles, no trail connects the two sections. Twenty miles of pavement separate New Fane and Greenbush.

The eight-kilometer Purple Loop at Greenbush dishes out hills and thrills as well as any trail in the Southern Kettles. Don't expect any technical singletrack, however. The beginning of the loop, which travels through red pine plantations, didn't impress us. Halfway through the loop, however, the ride gets interesting. First, the woods open up and allow a look-see at the surrounding countryside, dairy farms and silos in the distance. Then the hills rise and fall, twist and turn—the stuff we dream of riding. The short one-kilometer Pink Loop is an equally challenging trail, but it ends too quickly.

The backside of Purple runs directly past some small kettles, past Bear Lake and Bear Lake Marsh, nesting grounds for waterfowl. It winds past some massive oaks and through deep woods, reminiscent of up north. Near the end of the Purple Loop a sign warns novice skiers to take off skis and walk downhill—this is a good ride.

A note of caution: the Purple Loop is closed from the start of small game season through the end of gun deer season, roughly from the Chequamegon Fat Tire Festival (mid-September) until Thanksgiving. This leaves only the inner loops to ride during the peak of the autumn colors.

New Fane, on the other hand, was disappointing after Greenbush. The 5.2-kilometer Purple Loop ended much too quickly. The Red, Green, and Brown Loops (the DNR could use some help in their trail naming) run 4, 2.5, and 1.1 kilometers respectively. Not a lot of distance. The Red and Purple Loops run together on the backside through open fields and red pine plantations. The front side of these loops does travel through more typical kettle moraine terrain. Nevertheless, beginning and intermediate riders, and those who like to ride lap after lap, will enjoy New Fane. And it's close to Milwaukee.

Directions: The Greenbush Trails can be accessed from Kettle Moraine Drive, two and a half miles south of the town of Greenbush on Highway 23. The New Fane Trails are northeast of Kewaskum. County Highway S north out of Kewaskum runs into Kettle Moraine Drive once again, where you will turn right. Then turn left, or east, onto County Line Road. The parking lot is just off County Line Road. For more information contact the DNR office. Telephone is 920-626-2116, on weekends call 920-533-8222. Website is www.dnr.state.wi.us.

Fee: A Wisconsin Parks vehicle sticker and a trail pass are required.

Kettle Moraine State Forest

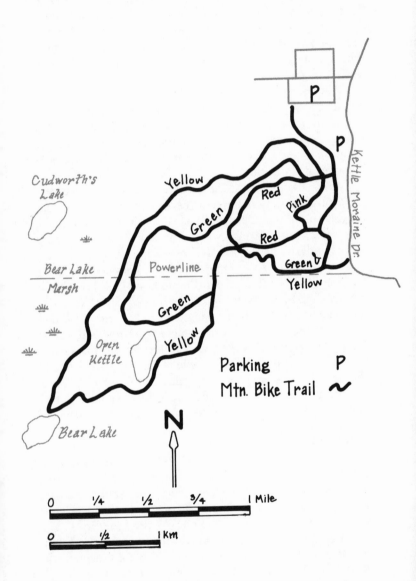

Cudworth's Lake

Yellow

Green

Red

Pink

Red

Green

Yellow

Kettle Moraine Dr.

P

P

Bear Lake Marsh

Powerline

Green

Yellow

Open Kettle

Bear Lake

Parking   P
Mtn. Bike Trail ~

N

0   1/4   1/2   3/4   1 Mile

0   1/2   1 Km

100

New Fane Trails

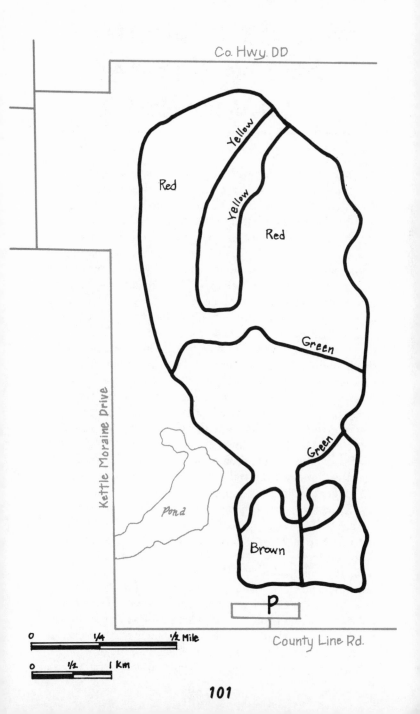

Co. Hwy. DD

Yellow

Yellow

Red

Red

Green

Kettle Moraine Drive

Green

Pond

Brown

P

County Line Rd.

0   ¼   ½ Mile

0   ½   1 Km

Kettle Moraine State Forest
Southern Unit

If you don't like crowds, stay away from the Kettles. On weekends, hordes of ATBers from nearby cities descend on the Southern Unit of the Kettle Moraine State Forest as though it were the last place on earth to ride. We had a hard time fighting through traffic—just in the parking lot. The trails were crowded as well. Every five minutes we were either passing or being passed by other riders. One fellow we'd never met before insisted on tagging along with us, silently begging us to dice it up with him the entire ten miles of the John Muir Trail's outer loops. A competitive fever hangs about the Kettles, especially on the weekends. Weekdays are more relaxed.

The Kettles is the most frequented trail system in the state. Thousands ride here every season. It's within an hour of Chicago, Milwaukee, and Madison, and riders visit for good reason. Described as singletrack, the trails are easily the most challenging in the southern half of Wisconsin. They climb and descend, winding all the while through the wooded and hilly kettle moraine topography. Although the trails aren't what we'd call true singletrack—bar-banging tight trail that squeezes through trees and around rocks and roots—they do challenge ATBers' skills, especially when ridden at race speed.

Riders can choose between the John Muir or Emma F. Carlin Trails, plus the five-mile-long connecting trail, which the DNR recently widened to control erosion, much to the dismay of local riders. The John Muir Trails feature five loops, from the mile and a half Red to the ten-mile Blue. Emma Carlin is smaller, consisting of only three loops: the Red (two miles), the Orange (two and a half miles), and the Green (four miles). Mountain biking is forbidden on all other trails in the Southern Unit. Most hikers stay on the hiking-only trails and the Ice Age Trail that runs the entire length of the state forest, although we nearly plowed into a startled couple on a blind

Levis/Trow Mounds

When we pulled into the lot at Levis/Trow Mounds, the buzzards were waiting, a lone pair wheeling fifty feet above Highway 95 so close we could see the gaps between their black and white feathers. Did the turkey buzzards know something that we didn't?

Levis Mound, a limestone butte rising three hundred feet above the surroundings, makes for exceptional buzzard country. And exceptional buzzard country makes for good mountain bike country. Local riders, members of the Neillsville Area Trail Association (NATA), have and continue to develop some of the best true singletrack in Wisconsin, over sixteen miles in total. We seem to ride new singletrack every time we visit, which is usually a couple times per year.

This often disheartening singletrack complements the nearly twenty kilometers of sandy doubletrack ski trails. Switchback Trail, a 2.2-kilometer deer trail up the side of Levis, might be the most difficult section here, relentlessly switching back and forth across the south face of the mound. In fact it's so difficult that each September Buzzard Buster race organizer Steve Meurett leaves this section out of the race. He doesn't want to be held responsible for possible carnage if he penciled Switchback into the race. Both ascending and descending this trail takes excellent bike-handling skills, as well as sheer horsepower for the climb up.

Much of the Levis/Trow singletrack cuts across the faces of both of these bluffs—off-camber trail with a long drop on one hand, and limestone rises overhead on the other hand. Gravity wants to pull the bike down through a maze of rock, red pine, and brush. This is definitely not a trail for the weak of heart. Or lung. At the top of Levis several scenic overlooks, dead end spurs off the main singletrack, offer views of the flat valley below, a valley that still looks much like it did two hun-

corner while riding Muir. The DNR recently built new mountain bike trails at Muir, yet even if they doubled the mileage at Muir, these trails would still be the most congested in the state.

The Emma Carlin Trails, north of Muir, see fewer riders, mainly because most ATBers park at Muir and don't ride the connecting trail between the two systems. Carlin is a more scenic and unyielding trail than Muir. The connecting trail used to be a gem, with three tricky rock- and root-strewn roller coaster hills, until its recent reconstruction. WORBA is working with the DNR, organizing and sponsoring work days to show officials that challenging, narrow trail can work, even at a highly trafficked destination like the Southern Kettles.

Plastic erosion control mats, necessary to protect the trail from the pounding of thousands of knobby tires, make climbing up the many steep climbs here difficult. Even the newest trails have been pounded into a hard boilerplate surface. In some spots, knobbies have eaten away the soil, exposing underlying rocks and increasing the chances for puncture. Bring along a spare tube or two and a pump.

Few of the trails run straight or flat at the Kettles. Our favorite section of trail winds along the top of an esker, a sharp glacial ridge on Carlin's Green Loop. The trail climbs a steep, rocky shoot to the top of the ridge, just after the connecting trail joins Carlin from the south. The views through the oaks show the surrounding forest and the flatlands beyond. To the north, the cathedral spires at Holy Hill are visible on a clear day.

Visit the La Grange General Store (telephone is 262-495-8600 and website is www.backyardbikes.com), a combination bike shop and cafe at the intersection of County Highway H and Highway 12 in La Grange, which features some great sandwiches, pasta salads, and local brews, as well as Gary Fisher bikes. For trailside snacks or repairs, check out the Artisan Cafe and Quiet Hut Sports on Bluff Road near the intersection of the connecting trail and Muir's Blue Loop.

Directions: Take County Highway H one and a half miles north from LaGrange. The Muir parking lot sits on the west side of the road. For information contact the Kettle Moraine State Forest–Southern Unit, S91W39091 Highway 59, Eagle, Wisconsin 53119. Telephone is 262-594-6200.

Fee: A Wisconsin Parks vehicle sticker and a trail pass are required.

Kettle Moraine State Forest

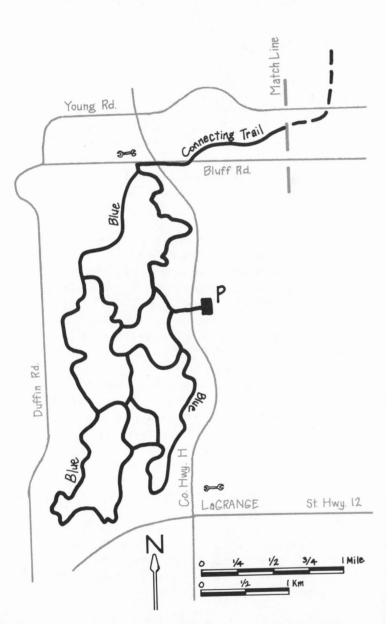

Young Rd.

Connecting Trail

Bluff Rd.

Blue

Blue

Blue

Duffin Rd.

Co. Hwy. H

Match Line

P

LaGRANGE   St. Hwy. 12

N

| 0 | ¼ | ½ | ¾ | 1 Mile |

| 0 | ½ | 1 Km |

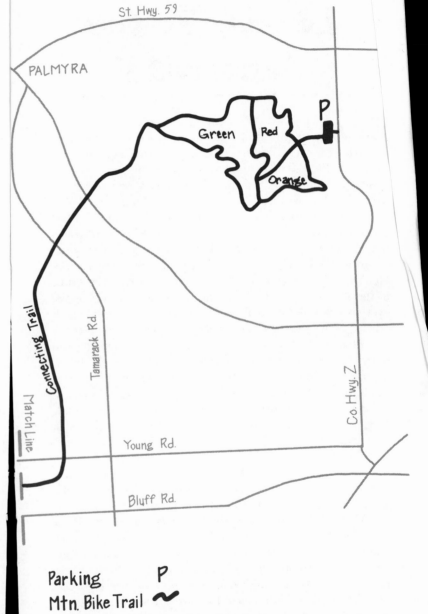

St. Hwy. 59

PALMYRA

Green   Red

Orange

P

Connecting Trail

Match Line

Tamarack Rd.

Co. Hwy. Z

Young Rd.

Bluff Rd.

Parking   P

Mtn. Bike Trail ~

dred years ago. Look for buzzards up here, spinning their magic. Local riders have seen as many as thirty riding the thermals, on the lookout for dinner. Or perhaps for mountain bikers busted up by the sheer force of the terrain. Besides the imperturbable buzzards, turkey, deer, black bear, coyote, and perhaps even a stray wolf roam the mounds.

Not all terrain at Levis is gut-wrenching terrain, although beginning riders should start somewhere not so challenging. Three mild doubletrack loops circle the mounds. The Levis Loop, the easiest at six and a half kilometers, circles Levis. The eight and a half kilometer Levis Loppet runs out in the flats between Levis and Trow Mounds. And the twelve and a half kilometer Moundbounder ends up circling both Trow and Levis Mounds. Most of the singletrack lies on or around Levis Mound, although NATA has recently completed two more miles of singletrack up and around Trow Mound. Right now, four singletrack trails tackle Trow: Buck Hill, Fox Hole Hill, Koch's Cooker, and Upper Hermosa—all with tough climbs. Most riders, according to Meurett, tend to stay around Levis and few venture out to Trow, something he would like to see change.

Expect more new trail each year as NATA continues to develop their already wonderful system. Since the singletrack isn't marked as well as the doubletrack, you might want to try one of the NATA group rides or go with somebody familiar with the trails. NATA also holds short, but brutal, time trials during the season. Ask local riders about more singletrack at Wedges Creek, seven miles west of Neillsville on Highway 10.

Directions: Levis is located halfway between Black River Falls and Neillsville on Highway 95. For more information write NATA, W7622 Arndt Road, Neillsville, Wisconsin, 54456.

Fee: A daily fee can be paid at the drop box at the trailhead.

Levis and Trow Mound Trails

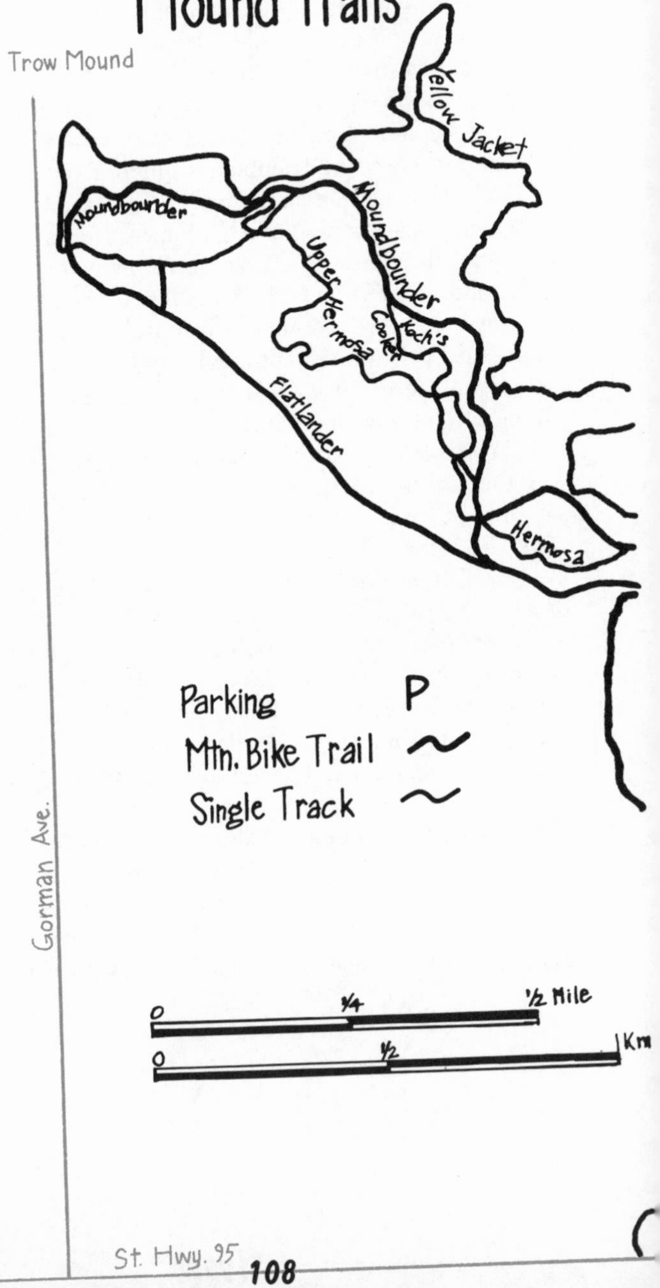
Trow Mound
Yellow Jacket
Moundbounder
Moundbounder
Upper Hermosa
Cooker
Koch's
Flatlander
Hermosa
Parking P
Mtn. Bike Trail
Single Track
Gorman Ave.
0
1/4
1/2 Mile
0
1/2
1 Km
St. Hwy. 95

Standing Rocks Trail

Standing Rocks Trail, southeast of Stevens Point, gets its name from the many giant boulders, technically called glacial erratics, which dot the area. The landscape seems scrunched up, like someone picked up the township by the corner and shook it until all the hills, valleys, and big rocks crowded together at one end. Riding a bike amid this jumble can be daunting. Most of the hills aren't long, but they are steep. Add a sandy, loose soil and you have a recipe for aching quadriceps and burning lungs.

The thirteen or so miles of trails are wide and well-marked, but the ones called Oak Ridge Run and Logger's Loop still get confusing. These are farthest from the trailhead and twist through an area recently butchered for its white oak. The best tree scenery is found on Lodge Loop (also called the Green Trail). It's only about one kilometer long and a fine place for ripping off a few warm-up laps.

Although the trails are well-marked, trying to follow them by their various names can be confusing. Signs at most intersections have "you are here" marks. Both the Red and Blue Trails are consistently marked with same-color diamonds. Picking a color and riding it avoids the confusion of all the trail names.

The longer Blue Trail incorporates Red Pine Run, Ice Age Loop, Tower Road, Oak Ridge Run, and Logger's Loop. Approximately ten kilometers in length, this trail makes a great ride. We headed out from the parking lot to Red Pine Run. One of the two largest downhills in the system dropped off immediately. The run is straight and requires no technical skill, only comfort with downhill speed. The next two kilometers reclaim the altitude lost down the big hill. Your granny-gears will come in handy here.

The run down to Tower Road is straight and fast, but the intersection at the bottom requires some caution, as bikers and even cars can be in the way. Turn right on the road, head north a couple hundred meters and then make a left onto Oak Ridge Run. This maze-like concoction of loops within loops can be fun. Stay with the blue diamonds to do the entire ten kilometers. There are lots of little, fast hills with equally many tight turns. Loose sand adds to the excitement, and to the pain.

Exiting this area we discovered the second significant hill on the Blue Trail. It's straight and not demanding technically, but like the first hill, it is long and steep. A long gradual climb took us back up into a red pine plantation and the intersection with the trail back to the parking lot. A right turn and then a steep climb brought us to the downhill ski area.

This small downhill area, complete with tow rope, operates in the winter. The view from the top of the hill, down to Bear Lake, is captivating. Cycling on the grassy downhill slopes isn't allowed. Instead, follow the trail out around the downhill area and toward Red Pine Run, where a sharp right turn takes the trail down a long, steep descent to the lakeshore. The trail hugs the boggy shoreline on the west side of the lake. We tried riding it, but a pair of Canada geese protecting their nest threatened us with pecking damage, so we turned around. We climbed back up the hill and found it less enjoyable but no less a challenge.

Directions: From the junction of Highway 51 and County Highway B in Plover, go east four and a half miles on County B to Custer Road, then turn right and go about a mile and quarter to Standing Rocks Road. Go left one and a half miles to the park entrance on the left.

Fee: Portage County requires a $5 trail fee. They also enforce the fee, so pay before riding.

Standing Rocks Trails

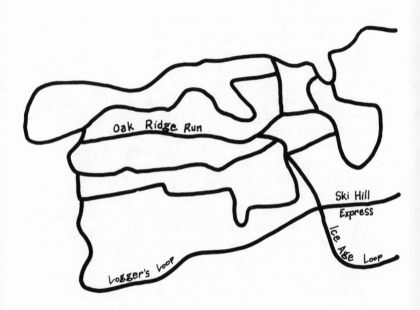

Oak Ridge Run

Ski Hill
Express

Ice Age Loop

Logger's Loop

Standing Rocks Rd.

Tower Rd. Trail

Ice Age Loop

Red Pine Run

Lake Shore Stride

Bear Lake

P Chalet

N

Lodge Loop

Standing Rocks Rd.

Parking   P

Mtn. Bike Trail ~

0   1/4   1/2 Mile

0   1/4   1/2   3/4   1 Km

113

Levis/
Trow ★
Mounds
  ★
Black River

Standing Rocks ★

Northern Kettles ★

Governor Dodge
  ★

Southern Kettles
  ★

The
Southern
Shorts

Area 25.5

Wouldn't it be something if there was a trail system connecting bluffs and valleys of the farm country west of Madison? Unfortunately, almost all of this land is private. Fortunately, there are some farmers and landowners in the area sympathetic to mountain biking.

West of Pine Bluff, WORBA has built some of the most technical singletrack in the state on two small sections of private land. Called Area 25.5, these trails are entirely singletrack—no roads (unless we count the pavement that connects the two sections) no ski trail, no doubletrack. Just narrow, winding, climbing trails that meander up and down heavily wooded bluffs. One trail snakes around one of the largest oaks we've encountered in a while. We used our granny-gears to get up most of the climbs and pushed our bikes up the few we couldn't climb. On the descents, we never left the middle chainring because the trail is too tight to allow much speed.

The WORBA trails are marked with orange surveyor's tape, but once you find the trails they're obvious. These trails run on private land, so tread lightly and ride respectfully. We're sorry we can't provide explicit directions to Area 25.5. One must be a WORBA member and be willing to put in eight hours of trail maintenance to ride here. It's worth it. For more information on this trail and becoming a WORBA member, contact them at P.O. Box 1681, Madison, Wisconsin 53701-1681 or www.worba.org.

Badger Prairie County Park

This Dane County park is aptly named—at least the prairie part. We didn't run into any badgers, though. With the exception of a short singletrack section on the high ground surrounding the Verona water tower, the few miles of trails here are wide swaths mowed through the prairie. Consequently, the trails are neither hilly nor technical, making it a good place for a family to ride. The Ice Age hiking trails wind through the park, and bicyclists can get on the Military Ridge Trail just outside the entrance to the park—another bonus for family riding.

The prairie does have its moments: the day we rode here the wild mustard was blooming, its yellow punctuating the dominating green of the June prairie, and dozens of meadowlarks piped and cavorted in the warm breezes. These trails are also close to Madison's many metro mountain bikers.

Directions: Badger Prairie is just north of the Dane County Care Center on old Highway 151. There is $2 daily or $15 yearly fee. Telephone is 608-246-3896 or 608-242-4576.

Bluebird Springs Recreational Area

Bluebird Springs hosted one of the earliest mountain bike races in Wisconsin, back in the days when people took the mountain in mountain biking seriously. The trails that climb up and down the Mississippi River bluffs here just east of La Crosse are the most aerobically difficult in this book. They plain hurt.

After a few years the Bluebird race faded. Maybe it was too difficult, who knows. But in 1997 the old race was revived and inserted in the Wisconsin Off-Road Series (WORS) and given a new name (The Crusty Bluff Hunker Down). Interestingly, it's subtitled the Revenge of the Bluebird Springs Recreation Area. If there's one race that eats racers alive, it's the Crusty Bluff, which is why the promoters claim that "this is the toughest course you'll ride all year, the one you will love and hate."

In 1998, the course featured three one-mile-long climbs per seven-mile loop. Three gut-wrenching, leg-burning granny-gear climbs. When you can no longer pedal that tiny gear, you get off and push. This is real mountain biking. Once at the top, the challenge doesn't end. The descent down these limestone-strewn trails can be as nasty as the grind uphill.

Bluebird does feature some milder riding in the fifteen or so kilometers of trail here. Riders can avoid most of the big climbs by sticking to the old logging roads that run the creek bottoms of the Smith Valley where Bluebird is located. It's also here in the valley where riders can find the choice camping sites. For more information about them call 608-781-CAMP.

Directions: From I-90 take Highway 16 south to County Highway B. Turn left, or east, on County B and go two miles to Smith Valley Road, which dead ends at Bluebird.

Fee: Two dollars per day, what a bargain.

Blue Mound State Park

Currently a five-mile trail used mainly for cross-country skiing runs through the state park and ultimately connects with the Military Ridge State Trail. WORBA is hoping to add five to eight miles of singletrack in the state park, which would be a blessing for the growing number of downstate mountain bikers, particularly in the Madison area. The proposed singletrack would complement the existing doubletrack which traverses the Blue Mound, the highest point in the state south of Rib Mountain.

The new trail will use the north and west portions of the park, an area of ravines that was struck by the 1984 tornado that ripped apart the nearby town of Barneveld, including Mark's uncle's house a block south of Main Street. For information contact Karl Heil, the park manager, at 608-437-5771.

Calumet County Park

This county park sits along the eastern shore of Lake Winnebago, about three miles south of the more popular High Cliff State Park. As at High Cliff, the Niagara Escarpment slices through the park, giving the eastern shore the most vertical relief in the area.

Lawrence Martin, in his classic *Physical Geography of Wisconsin*, says the steep slope that runs up the eastern side of the state is "known locally as the Ledge." Around the northeastern shores of Lake Winnebago "the escarpment descends abruptly to the lake." At High Cliff it falls 233 feet, and just a few miles south of Calumet County Park the escarpment drops 313 feet. With all this vertical relief, the county runs a tubing and sledding hill in winter, and in the other seasons people can camp, boat, swim, hike, and mountain bike at the park.

In July, WORBA's Fox Valley Chapter organizes a WORS race here, which in 1998 drew over 1,300 participants. The race uses just about every bit of the vertical in the park that rises up from Lake Winnebago.

All totaled, Calumet has approximately five miles of trail, including a few short sections of tricky singletrack. Some of the climbs, over two hundred vertical feet, might require a granny-gear. One of the trails on the escarpment runs along-

118

side three ancient effigy mounds. Calumet County Park has seventy-one campsites, most with electricity.

Directions: The park is north of Stockbridge on Highway 55. Turn west on County Highway EE to the park entrance. For information contact the Calumet County Park, N6150 County Highway EE, Hilbert, Wisconsin 54129. Telephone is 920-439-1008 and e-mail is 1009ccp@fox.tds.net.

Cam-Rock County Park

Cam-Rock, another Dane County park, consists of three hundred or so acres clustered in three separate areas along the Rockdale Millpond, home to several pairs of Canada geese. Area Two, just off County Highway B, has a couple miles of mild doubletrack, cross-country ski trails in winter, and has hosted the Wisconsin Cyclocross Championships several times. A few years back, Mark was winning a race here with a few laps to go when his seat fell off. He pressed on, but victory slipped away. He did find out that riding off-road is difficult without a seat.

Area Three, north of the hamlet of Rockdale off Highland Drive, has two short sections of WORBA-built singletrack. This is our favorite section there and was featured in a grand opening ceremony in June of 2000. Sections 3E and 3W snake up and down the only real elevation at Cam-Rock above the millpond. Section 3W is the more technical as it makes its way through some loose limestone and down into dry creek bottoms. Both demand moderate bike-handling skills.

All totaled, Cam-Rock has perhaps ten kilometers of trail, so experienced riders might get bored quickly here. The surrounding countryside is beautiful, however (we rode around a bit on the pavement), and nearby Cambridge is widely known for its antique shopping. The Night Heron, an endearing brick home in Rockdale, offers bed and breakfast accommodations.

Directions: Take County Highway B southwest out of Cambridge. The park is on the north side of the road. Daily or yearly fees can be paid at a drop box at the trailhead. Telephone is 608-246-3896 or 608-242-4576.

Devil's Head Resort

Downstate ATBers are raving about the twenty-six kilometers of trail that officially opened here in June of 1995. The trails that crisscross the eight hundred acres at the downhill ski resort range from easy to difficult. The toughest trails tackle the ski hills on the Wisconsin River bluffs overlooking nearby Merrimac and the surrounding valley. The Badger State Games has held its yearly mountain bike competition here on the south-facing slopes, utilizing the difficult climbs and the twisting singletrack descents. This development echoes others across the country: ski resorts are opening their arms and their slopes to mountain bikers. Budget Bicycle of Madison operates a rental and repair facility at the resort. A $7 daily trail fee is required—you have to pay to play.

Directions: From Merrimac take Bluff Road three miles to Devil's Head. The ferry across the Wisconsin River at Highway 113 is worth the wait. It's also free. Telephone is 800-472-6670.

Devil's Lake State Park

This is a place of long climbs and long descents. Begin riding from the parking area off County Highway DL. Take the Ice Age Loop, which parallels the road for almost a kilometer. The first few hundred meters is through open field on mostly flat terrain. As trees close in around the trail, it starts climbing. There's another kilometer of ups and downs until the trail starts a long ascent up to the top of the east bluff. Huff and puff and enjoy the view from one of the rock ledges.

Then get ready to descend. The pitch is mild at first. Crank if you like. The second pitch is rough and tough. Most riders will need to stay close to their brakes. Gravel makes the speed dangerous, but exciting. Toward the end of the run a right turn heads the trail down one more serious descent, this one long but straight.

At the next intersection the trail goes straight back out to the field and the parking lot, or turns left and makes a loop ending with a swoop down one last hill to the field.

Directions: From Highway 123 south of Baraboo, take County Highway DL about a mile and a half east of the main park entrance. There is parking on the south side of DL. For information contact Devil's Lake State Park, S5975 Park Road, Baraboo, Wisconsin 53913. Telephone is 608-356-8301.

High Cliff State Park

Expect easy, non-technical riding here, but as one friend says referring to the Fox Valley area, "It's all we got over here." Although the eight miles of trail that wind along the Niagara Escarpment, a ridge two hundred feet above Lake Winnebago, won't challenge experienced riders, the trail does travel through some nicely wooded areas with views of Wisconsin's largest inland lake. The trails are typical of state parks—wide enough for the DNR to patrol by pickup. An excellent choice for a low-keyed cruise.

Directions: From Appleton take Highway 114 six miles east to State Park Road. For information contact High Cliff State Park, N7475 High Cliff Road, Menasha, Wisconsin 54952. Telephone is 920-989-1349.

Kickapoo Valley Reserve

Over thirty years ago, Wisconsin Senator William Proxmire pushed Congress into authorizing a dam on the Kickapoo River near La Farge. Like many such projects, the proposed dam raised many economic, environmental, as well as social concerns, such as the displacement of about 140 farm families living in the valley. After cost overruns, construction was halted in 1975.

The question then—who would control the approximately 8,500 acres? The county? The state? The federal government? Or even the Ho-Chunk Nation? Ultimately, the state was granted control of most of these acres, although the Ho-Chunk do control about 1,200 acres with cultural and historical importance.

Currently, the KVR Board is managing the state's land and is still in the process of deciding which groups—hikers, equestrians, snowmobilers, mountain bikers—get what. In short, everybody is still fighting for a piece of the pie.

There are ten miles of mountain bike trails in the KVR, with the potential for many more miles, especially singletrack. What is here is mostly doubletrack that climbs up and down the steep hills the Kickapoo Valley and the Driftless Area are famous for. A few of the hardwood hills rise over six hundred feet above the valley, so there is plenty of vertical here for the climbers.

Since the trails are in the process of evaluation, ride wisely. A few of the trails—near Hay Valley and Wolf Roads—run contiguous with the equestrian trails. Don't spook the horses. Also, be alert for hikers. We might see more trail if we ride responsibly and demonstrate the economic impact of our sport.

Camping is available in the KVR and also at Wildcat Mountain State Park, just north of the Reserve. Free permits (so the management can evaluate usage) are available at the La Farge office. Trails are open from the first of May to the fifteenth of November, but may be temporarily shut down because of wet weather.

Directions: The KVR is north of La Farge, which sits at the intersection of Highways 82 and 131. The main office is just off 131 at the northern end of town. For information contact the Kickapoo Valley Reserve, 505 North Mill Street, La Farge, Wisconsin 54639. Telephone is 608-625-2906 and website is http://kvr.state.wi.us/static/.

Lapham Peak State Forest

Known mostly as one of the best spots to cross-country ski in Wisconsin, this section of the Kettle Moraine State Forest does allow mountain biking on certain trails, nearly five miles total. The trails are wide and flat to rolling, avoiding the steep verticals that the Kettle Moraine landscape is famous for. Park officials and skiers are worried that mountain bikes on the steeper trails will cause erosion, and we tend to agree. The ski trail up to the observation tower is closed to riding, but it's perhaps worth a hike to view the surrounding countryside.

Call ahead before riding here. Lapham Peak is often closed for several days after a rain to allow the trails to dry out.

Directions: From I-94 west of Milwaukee take County Highway C south about one mile. You should be able to see the tower from the interstate. For information contact Lapham Peak Unit, Kettle Moraine State Forest, N846 W329 County Highway C, Delafield, Wisconsin 53018. Telephone is 262-646-3025.

Mirror Lake State Park

The seven miles of trail open to ATBs runs through oak and pine woods. Occasional sand blows make interesting forms in the otherwise forested landscape. The hills aren't difficult save for an occasional patch of soft sand. A new WORBA chapter is dedicated to improving and maintaining the trails here and has plans for new singletrack.

The three segments comprising the system are linked together like sausages, with easy access to each link from any of the various road crossings. Look for upcoming singletrack, compliments of the new Mirror Lake WORBA Chapter, which is dedicated to improving the trails and the mountain biking experience here.

Directions: From I-90/94 exit Highway 12 south, nineteen miles west of the Portage exit. Go one mile to Fern Dell Road. Turn west and the park headquarters is on the right. For information contact Mirror Lake State Park, E10320 Fern Dell Road, Baraboo, Wisconsin 53913. Telephone is 608-254-2333.

Nepco Lake Trail

Wisconsin Rapids, lying in the broad, sandy valley of the Wisconsin River, doesn't seem to be a likely place to find decent riding. The area seems too flat, too swampy. Appearance can be deceiving, however.

The area around Nepco Lake, on the southern edge of the city, has some wonderful singletrack. Miles of it, in fact. Outside of locals who blazed much of the trail, few riders know about this hidden gem.

Start at the YMCA Camp, south of Griffith State Nursery on the west side of Highway 13. Take off on the doubletrack and look for the singletrack. Unfortunately, none of this trail is mapped or marked since it's unofficial trail, much of it on Georgia Pacific land. The trail here winds up, down, and around gullies and washes emptying into Nepco Lake. Jack pine and scrub oak have rooted into the sandy soil.

On the other side of Highway 13 look for more trail along the southern shores of the lake. The trail here is even more technical than that at the YMCA Camp. Take Townline Road east and immediately look for singletrack on the left, leading north into the woods. Talk to the people at Bring's Cyclery (715-423-5520 or brings74@hotmail.com) on 8th Street South, who can provide even more detailed directions for these sandy trails.

Directions: Nepco Lake is a half mile south of Wisconsin Rapids on Highway 13.

Perrot State Park

This state park is unique in a lot of ways. From Brady's Bluff it offers perhaps the best view of the Mississippi River valley north of Wyalusing State Park (the Brady's Bluff Trail is a hike-only trail). It has broad expanses of native prairie, near-state-record circumference black ash and black walnut trees, and the confluence of the Mississippi and Trempealeau Rivers. Effigy mounds dot the campground. The park is also home to the only gopher-excavated bike trail we rode during our entire research for this book—or ever for that matter. If you've never ridden a gopher riddled trail, it's a teeth-chattering, bone-bouncing experience. Had we actually come across one of the furry little creatures, we would have run it down with glee. The Bay Trail, home to the industrious gophers, starts on the east side of the campground and provides a couple of decent views of Trempealeau Bay and Trempealeau Mountain beyond. The bay is home to thousands of waterfowl during the summer. We rode the trails at Perrot in mid-October, after duck hunting season had begun, and didn't see a single bird.

By far the best biking at Perrot starts just behind the park office. The ride begins with a respectable climb up to what's called White Pine Run. We found a fourteen-foot circumference basswood tree hugging the trail on the left. White Pine Run is wide and smooth. Just when we were wondering when the climbing would start we hit Tow Rope Hill. While lots of cross-country skiers have wished for a tow, we peddled our quads off then still had to walk the second half of the hill. The trail undulates for the next mile or so, never taking away all the altitude gained on Tow Rope, yet rushing down a couple of hills and climbing back up a couple.

Then we hit Ski Jump Hill, a very deceptive little drop. Initially it seemed overnamed, nothing much, but suddenly there was a ledge, a precipice that didn't allow a view beyond. Brakes squeaked and eyes widened as we went over the edge, wondering what awaited. The steep drop was short, about thirty yards, but then the more gradually pitched, twisting Valley Run continued, and continued, and then continued. Somewhere between the second and third continue, eroded ruts started appearing in the trail, mostly diagonal to the trail, but angled at whatever cant the fall line water had decided was the fastest way down during the last major rainstorm. Eyes widened again, brakes squealed, and in one case, feet came out of toe-clips and pedals just prior to an imagined crash.

After Valley Run the ride back around Cedar Glade was tame. We took in one incredible view. Rounding Perrot Ridge a meadow stretches to the west and partly up Brady's Bluff. The meadow is covered with native prairie. We saw waves of tan indian grass, spotted with a few light blue asters and yellow goldenrod. Dark green juniper topped with golden aspen framed the meadow. The trail connects with White Pine Run shortly after the meadow. Stay to the right as you retrace your tracks back to the start at the park office because there's one more thrill waiting. Called Da Chute by folks at the park, it's a quick drop off the bluff to the parking lot.

Directions: From the intersection of Highways 35 and 53 north of La Crosse, take 35 North (southwest at this point) eight miles to Trempealeau. Follow the signs to Perrot State Park. For information contact Perrot State Park, Route 1, Box 407, Trempealeau, Wisconsin 54661. Telephone is 608-534-6409.

Quarry Park

This Madison park is maybe the one place in this book that really isn't a destination. There's no official parking lot, and most people ride here. No cars, no racks. The Quarry Park is a neighborhood place in the middle of Mad City.

For that reason it attracts a different crowd, the freeride crowd if you will: kids, mostly BMXers, and urban riders. Tattoos, dual-suspended bikes, loud music, chains on wallets as well as bikes. Eric Lynn, a graphic designer for Fisher and Bontrager, says, "You don't see a lot of spandex at the Quarry." Riders come here to see how far they can jump their bikes or see how fast they can shred the singletrack.

Lynn describes the layout of the trails as if "somebody took a big plate of spaghetti and dumped it out." The trails crisscross and intersect often as they weave through the few acres here just off University Avenue. Expect potholes, craters large enough to swallow bike and rider, and narrow trails with little margin for error.

This isn't a place to go for an aerobic workout. Rather, it's a place to ride to sharpen technical skills and maybe meet some interesting folks. Lynn rides the quarry because it has a "neat soul of its own."

Directions: Quarry Park is behind Whole Foods on University Avenue, but don't park in their lot if you do drive here. Turn south onto Hill Street where it intersects University Avenue and park on Harvey Street.

Yellow River State Forest

Yes, this state forest is in Iowa. It's probably closer to a lot of readers, however, than some of the trails way up north. Besides, from the bluffs in Yellow River you can see Wisconsin just across the Mississippi—that's close enough for us to include it in our book.

Yellow River has two units worth riding—Paint Creek, home of the park's main office, and Luster Heights, home of the Luster Heights Correctional Facility, a minimum security prison. Look for the brown sign to Luster Heights off Highway 364; the trails are only about a hundred yards away. The Luster Heights cross-country ski trails meander along a bluff overlooking Old Man River. These doubletrack trails present few technical difficulties, but the view down to the river three hundred feet below and across to Wisconsin is one of the best in the Midwest.

More cross-country ski trails await at Paint Creek, plus snowmobile/ATV trails and low maintenance logging roads.

Yes, they do log in Iowa, surprisingly enough in the corn and hog state. The logging road past the main office leads up a long climb to a fire tower, an out of place structure in the Hawkeye State and one of only a few. This road eventually travels out of the Paint Creek Unit and intersects Highway 364. A right on 364 leads back to the road to Luster.

The ski trails at Paint Creek are clustered in and around the bluff the fire tower graces. An abandoned railway runs along the north shore of Paint Creek, just north of the office and visitor center, and intersects Allamakee County Road X42. North of the creek several miles of snowmobile trails wind up into and along the Paint Creek bluffs. Unfortunately, many of these trails dead end. Nevertheless, they are worth riding.

Yellow River offers many camping sites. Check out those along Paint Creek (bring a fly rod for trout fishing) and the walk-in site at Brown's Hollow along the road that runs past the fire tower. Effigy Mounds National Monument, with its ancient Native American burial mounds shaped like eagles, bears, and other animals, is also worth visiting. Effigy Mounds lies on Highway 76 south of Paint Creek and Highway 364.

Directions: Take Highway 76 north from Marquette, Iowa, past Effigy Mounds. Right on Allamakee County Road X42. For information contact Yellow River State Forest, Park Ranger, Box 164A, Harpers Ferry, Iowa 52146. Telephone is 319-586-2548.

Index

Index

American beech, 49
Antigo, Wis., 84
Anvil Trail, 2–3, 44
Arbor Vitae, Wis., 45
Area 25.5, 116

Badger Prairie County Park, 116–17
Bad River, 34
Baird Creek, 78
bald eagles, 38, 40
Baraboo, Wis., 121, 123
Barneveld, Wis., 118
Bayfield, Wis., 40, 41
Bear Lake, 99
Bear Paw Inn, 78–79
Bear Trap Inn, 18
Beaver Lake, 42
Berkhahn Rookery Bicycle Loop, 79, 80
Big Eau Pleine County Park, 80
Birch Lake, 27
Birkebeiner Trail, 6, 7, 33
black ash, 124
black bear, 107
Black River Falls, Wis., 91
Black River State Forest, 90–91
black walnut, 124
bloodroot, 53
blue asters, 125
Blueberry Lake, 22
Bluebird Springs Recreational Area, 117
Blue Hills, 32
Blue Mound State Park, 118
bluewing teal, 79

Boulder Area Trail System (BATS), 37, 38
Boulder Junction, Wis., 11, 15, 39, 40
Brown County Reforestation Camp, 80–81
Brownstone Falls, 34
Bruce, Wis., 32
Brunsweiler River, 36, 42
Buckatabon Creek, 34
buzzards, 106, 107

Cable, Wis., 27, 34, 42
Calumet County Park, 118–19
Cambridge, Wis., 119
Cam-Rock County Park, 119
Canada geese, 79, 111
Chain of Lakes Cyclery, 3
Chequamegon Area Mountain Bike Association (CAMBA), xii, 6, 7, 19, 20, 26, 27, 32–34, 42, 44, 72
Chequamegon National Forest, 35, 36, 41, 42, 85
Chippewa Falls, Wis., 85
Church of Atonement, 57
Cisco Lake, 33
Civilian Conservation Corps (CCC), 2
Clam Lake, Wis., 35, 36, 42
Clark County Forest, 60, 61
Concrete Park, 43
Cooper's Hawks, 3, 81
Copper Falls State Park, 34, 41
cormorants, 48, 79
Cox Hollow Lake, 94